"The doctrine of the existence of spirits is established in nature; where those spirits reside, is a matter of difficulty, and our speculations are various about them; but to argue that therefore there are none, that they exist not, that there are no such beings, is absurd, and contrary to the nature of the thing; we may as well argue against the existence of the sun, when it is clouded and eclipsed, though we see its light, only because we cannot see its beams, or the globe of its body."

—Daniel Defoe, *An Essay on the History and Reality of Apparitions*

GHOST UNDER FOOT

ABOUT THE AUTHOR

Kenneth W. Harmon lives in Fort Collins, Colorado, with his wife and four daughters. A retired police officer, Kenneth now writes full time. A prior finalist for the Pacific Northwest Writer's Association Zola Award, he has been published in numerous anthologies and online journals. For more, visit www.kennethwharmon.com.

TO WRITE TO THE AUTHOR

If you wish to contact the author or would like more information about this book, please write to the author in care of Llewellyn Worldwide Ltd., and we will forward your request. Both the author and the publisher appreciate hearing from you and learning of your enjoyment of this book and how it has helped you. Llewellyn Worldwide Ltd. cannot guarantee that every letter written to the author can be answered, but all will be forwarded. Please write to:

Kenneth W. Harmon
℅ Llewellyn Worldwide
2143 Wooddale Drive
Woodbury, MN 55125-2989

Please enclose a self-addressed stamped envelope for reply, or $1.00 to cover costs. If outside the USA, enclose an international postal reply coupon.

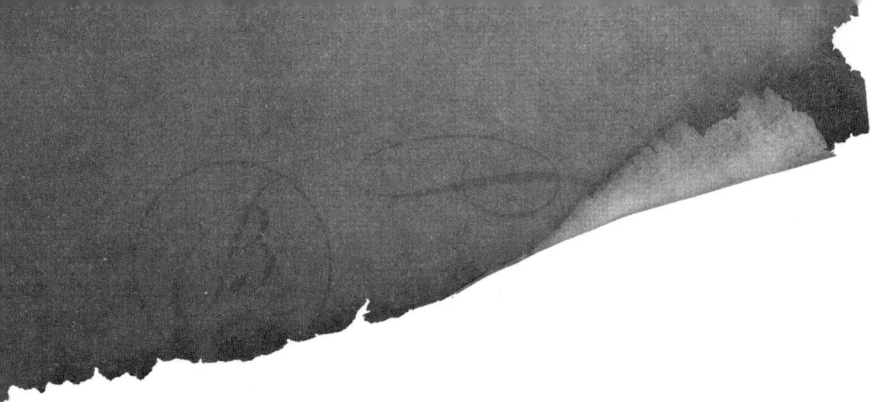

GHOST UNDER FOOT
The Spirit of Mary Bell

A TRUE STORY OF ONE FAMILY'S HAUNTING

KENNETH W. HARMON

Llewellyn Publications
Woodbury, Minnesota

Ghost Under Foot: The Spirit of Mary Bell © 2012 by Kenneth W. Harmon. All rights reserved. No part of this book may be used or reproduced in any manner whatsoever, including Internet usage, without written permission from Llewellyn Publications, except in the case of brief quotations embodied in critical articles and reviews.

First Edition
First Printing, 2012

Book design by Bob Gaul
Cover art: Forest © iStockphoto.com/Evgeny Kuklev
　　　　　Parchment © iStockphoto/Alex Max
　　　　　Woman © iStockphoto.com/Iconogenic
Interior Art: Parchment © iStockphoto/Alex Max
Cover design and illustration by Kevin R. Brown
Editing by Ed Day

Llewellyn is a registered trademark of Llewellyn Worldwide Ltd.

Library of Congress Cataloging-in-Publication Data
Harmon, Kenneth W., 1961-
　Ghost under foot : the Spirit of Mary Bell : a true story of one family's haunting/Kenneth W. Harmon.—1st ed.
　　p. cm.
　ISBN 978-0-7387-3081-3
1. Harmon, Kenneth W., 1961- 2. Spiritualism—Case studies. 3. Mary Bell, 1864-1886 (Spirit) I. Title.
　BF1283.H326A3 2012
　133.1'2978868—dc23
　　　　　　　　　　　　　2011040300

Llewellyn Worldwide Ltd. does not participate in, endorse, or have any authority or responsibility concerning private business transactions between our authors and the public.

　All mail addressed to the author is forwarded, but the publisher cannot, unless specifically instructed by the author, give out an address or phone number.

　Any Internet references contained in this work are current at publication time, but the publisher cannot guarantee that a specific location will continue to be maintained. Please refer to the publisher's website for links to authors' websites and other sources.

Llewellyn Publications
A Division of Llewellyn Worldwide Ltd.
2143 Wooddale Drive
Woodbury, MN 55125-2989
www.llewellyn.com

Printed in the United States of America

CONTENTS

Acknowledgments ... XI

Prologue ... XIII

Chapter One ... 1

Chapter Two ... 5

Chapter Three ... 11

Chapter Four ... 33

Chapter Five ... 45

Chapter Six ... 57

Chapter Seven ... 67

Chapter Eight ... 83

Chapter Nine ... 91

Chapter Ten ... 115

Chapter Eleven ... 129

Chapter Twelve ... 139

Chapter Thirteen ... 155

Chapter Fourteen ... 167

Chapter Fifteen ... 203

Chapter Sixteen ... 213

Epilogue ... 217

Appendix ... 241

ACKNOWLEDGMENTS

This book would not have been possible without the help and support of many people to whom I owe thanks. My parents for their love and wisdom. My wife Monika for her love and support. My daughters Sarah, Michelle, Amanda, and Rebecca, who always manage to bring a smile to my face. My friend Darrin Mason, who has supported me and believed in me for many years. The members of the Penpointers and Raintree Writers, especially April Joitel Moore and Ross Willard, whose enthusiasm helped to motivate me. Duane and Susan Kniebes for sharing their knowledge. J. Allan Danelek and Mark Macy for their expert advice. Pat Walker at the Fort Collins Museum, who went above the call of duty to help me with research. Robert Larson and Carol Stetser from the Larimer County Genealogical Society who also contributed significantly to my research. Historians Cecilia Damschroder and the late Arlene Briggs Ahlbrandt.

Charles Burchett, who shared his knowledge of the history of the Harmony District. Dawn Allen, who shared her knowledge of ghosts and the paranormal. Amy Glaser, for believing in the project and for her editing.

PROLOGUE

The knocking on the headboard boomed inside my brain. I stopped breathing, my body paralyzed with fear, as I realized I was not alone in my room. I tried to remain calm. In my twelve years as a police officer, I had faced many dangers. A man once shot at me from the cover of darkness; another charged at me with a butcher knife. None of this prepared me for what I now experienced.

I sensed a presence inside the room, the ghost of a woman who had been dead for more than 120 years. She climbed onto the bed on my wife's side and slowly inched toward me. Thoughts of jumping out of bed and running came to me. The spirit moved closer. My heart raced. Sweat bubbled across my brow. Blood pounded through my ears. Then she reached me and laid down, a heavy weight that crushed my legs. This sensation lasted for perhaps a minute before the pressure gradually diminished. My chest heaved as I started to breathe once more.

I turned around to retrieve the video camera positioned behind me on the headboard. After rewinding the tape, I watched to see what, if anything, appeared on the video. I saw myself climb into bed, and orbs started to fly above me. When my daughter Amanda entered the room four minutes later, the orbs stopped, only to resume once she left, and I had returned to bed. Eight minutes into the tape, an orb flew past me in the direction of the headboard. Two seconds later, I heard the knocking, followed by silence as I held my breath.

In the summer of 2007, my family discovered we had a ghost living with us. I immediately launched an investigation into the phenomenon and gathered hours of video evidence along with hundreds of photographs. Ours is a ghost story, but it is not the Amityville Horror. Demons did not chase us from the house. Blood did not seep from the walls. This is a ghost story based on facts and supported by documented evidence, and it begins in a haunted hotel.

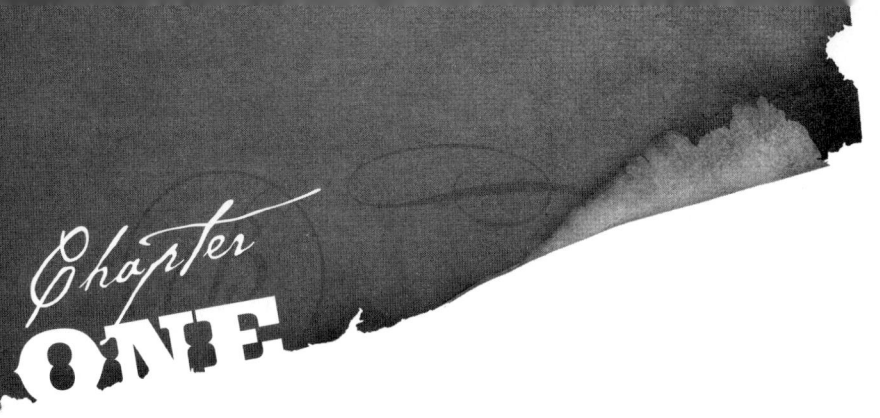

Chapter ONE

Most twenty-year-olds do not spend a lot of time thinking about death. I did. I had no choice. Less than a month after my twentieth birthday, I started classes at the Fort Worth police academy. Upon graduating in October 1981, I was the youngest officer on the force. Too young, in fact, to legally buy bullets for the gun I carried. When I began to patrol the streets, Fort Worth had the highest crime rate in the United States, according to FBI data, and the area of town I patrolled on the midnight shift had the highest crime rate in the city.

During my career with Fort Worth, I experienced the full range of human emotion and tragedy. One night a young woman died in my arms at the scene of a car accident. We had chased her inside a residential area after she fled from a traffic stop. She crashed her AMC Gremlin head on into a parked full-sized pickup truck, and she was not wearing a seatbelt. I ran up to her car and smelled gasoline. A week earlier, a car had crashed into a gas station in the nearby town of Forest Hills. While the Forest Hills police officer attempted to extract the driver, the car exploded, and the officer sustained fatal injuries. When I smelled the gasoline, my first thought was to get the girl out of the car before it exploded. I slipped my arms around her waist and managed to pull her upper body out of the car. I struggled to free her legs from under the crumpled dash, but it was no use. Soon the paramedics arrived. They had me continue to hold her as they fought to save her life. On another evening, I had to calm an angry father at John Peter Smith Hospital, whose five-year-old son lay dead in one of the emergency rooms, tortured and sexually abused by his ex-wife's boyfriend, his tiny body covered in cigarette burns.

Death is a constant companion when you work as a police officer. Between the murders, suicides, and accidents, I witnessed death on a weekly basis.

Our ideas regarding death change as we age. The first event that altered my view of death was the birth of my daughter Sarah. She developed pneumonia soon after she was born and for several days, the doctors were not sure if she would survive. Seconds ticked by slowly inside the hospital as my mind filled with more fear than

I thought possible. Fortunately, the doctors managed to diagnose Sarah's condition and start her on antibiotics. When I returned to work after Sarah's birth, I discovered that I had changed. Things I might have done in the past without concern for my personal safety now worried me. I thought about my own morality. What if I died? Who would take care of Sarah? As Sarah grew, I feared something happening to her. I could not imagine my life without her. My wife and I divorced when Sarah was eighteen months old. Sarah came to live with me and my fear of death increased, for now I was the one she counted on for everything.

I left the police department after twelve years and moved with Sarah to Washington State. At the age of thirty-nine, I remarried. My new wife Monika came from Indonesia. In 2000, we added a new daughter Michelle to the family, followed by Amanda and Rebecca. We were the typical American family. Our lives revolved around our kids. We watched all the new kid movies together as well as a fair share of cartoons on TV. I spent hours baking and decorating birthday cakes. In the summer of 2006, we took our first vacation. After visiting Big Bend National Park in Texas, we collided head on with a 1,200-pound bull while going 65 miles per hour, and walked away without a scratch. We fought and cried. We loved and laughed. And even though things did not always go as planned, we still had a grasp on where we were headed. The world made sense most of the time. That all changed in 2007 when events unfolded that shook the foundation upon which we had built our lives.

Chapter Two

I often joke that we are the Nomadic Harmons because we moved on average about every eight years. In 2004, we were residing in Henderson, Nevada. After seven and a half years in rainy Silverdale, Washington, Henderson seemed like paradise. The sun shined almost every day, and I even managed to ignore the scorching heat for a while. However, Henderson changed in the three years we lived there—thousands of new residents arrived each month, and after living in the natural beauty of Washington State, Henderson strip malls became a depressing sight. What we needed was to find a place that had the natural beauty of Silverdale but with better weather.

One day I was out shopping with Sarah, and we spotted a tent with a sign advertising used books for sale. We both love books, so the tent in the parking lot pulled us in like a magnet. After browsing for a while, I came across a book that rated the best places to retire in the United States. I thumbed through and read that Fort Collins, Colorado, ranked number one. Several years earlier, back when I used to drive up to Colorado from Texas to go skiing, I thought about moving there. I bought the book and hurried home to tell Monika about Fort Collins.

"This place is a college town with a population of about 130,000, with low crime, plenty of parks, and good schools. Old Town Fort Collins has shops and restaurants, plus the city nestles against the Rocky Mountain foothills, meaning there are things to do outdoors."

Monika folded her arms over her chest. "What's the weather like?"

"Fort Collins has four seasons."

This news brought a smile to her face. You might think that living in a place like Henderson, where the weather seldom changes, would be the greatest, but we were tired of the having the same weather every day.

"Why don't we visit Fort Collins over spring break?" I said.

Monika agreed. When I told my parents, who also lived in Henderson, about our plans, they decided to visit Fort Collins with us.

Arriving in Fort Collins was like a cool breeze across your face on a hot day. The midday sun perched over the

Rocky Mountains to the west. The temperature was crisp. We drove into Old Town Fort Collins and found the atmosphere a refreshing change from Henderson. It is not that we hated Henderson, but we needed somewhere quieter than the hustle and bustle of the Las Vegas Valley. I instantly fell in love with Fort Collins, as did Monika. When I informed my parents we were going to move, they followed our lead and started to look for a house.

We planned to move to Fort Collins in the first part of July, so toward the end of June, we returned to find a place to rent. We spent several days looking at rental houses without discovering a suitable one.

"Are we ever going to find a house?" Monika said, her tired eyes betraying frustration.

Sarah noticed a home for rent in the local paper. A new three-bedroom house, listed at $1,350 per month. After calling the owner, we arranged to see the house, located in the Linden Park Subdivision in southeast Fort Collins. When we pulled up to the two-story residence, it appeared like something from a Hawthorne novel, with a covered front porch and walkway flanked by half-stone columns. The paint was drab, a mix of gray and brown, with darker trim. The house sat in the middle of the block, and as we later discovered, received the least amount of sunlight of any house on the street. Still, after living in a cramped single-story house with a rock yard, this house was a huge upgrade.

When you enter, there is a room to your left with an eighteen-foot ceiling. This would be my office. The open stairwell is located close by. Continuing into the house, you pass a bathroom to the left before coming into the dining area and kitchen. The family room adjoins the dining area. Upstairs is a small landing. Three bedrooms and a bathroom connect to the landing. All the walls, doors, and baseboards were painted white, which gave the house a cold, almost clinical appearance. Only the dining room, entryway, stairwell, and bathrooms had overhead lights, a feature I never liked.

I conferred with my family, and we all agreed this house offered everything we needed, so we signed a rental agreement, and returned to Henderson for our stuff.

We settled into the new home quickly once we unpacked all of the boxes. We had no reason to believe a ghost might be living in the house. The house was new with no previous occupants. However, it was not long before strange things started to happen. Sarah approached me one evening, an uneasy expression on her face.

"Dad, whenever I go to bed, it feels as if someone is watching me."

She developed the habit of leaving the upstairs light on until she could turn on a light inside her bedroom.

I could have dismissed Sarah's concern as the product of an overactive teenage imagination, except both Monika and I had also experienced the feeling of someone watching us. In addition, Sarah had friends come over to visit who told her they sensed a presence inside the house.

Our poodle Rosie started to exhibit strange behavior. She liked to sleep on the back of the love seat in the family room. On several occasions, Rosie jumped up and took off running for no apparent reason. Rosie sleeps inside Sarah's room. One night she woke Sarah up with her growling. Rosie stood at the end of the bed, the hair up on her back, teeth bared. She stared at the closed bedroom door, a low threatening growl resonating from her chest. Sarah tried to quiet her, but Rosie would not stop growling. She finally scrambled under Sarah's bed and continued to growl. Sarah attempted to coax Rosie out, but she remained beneath the bed for the rest of the night. Another night, Rosie hunkered down at the top of the stairs and refused to cross the landing to go into Sarah's room. Sarah sat on her knees in the open doorway imploring Rosie to move, but Rosie held fast. Eventually, Sarah had to go over and pick Rosie up to carry her into her room.

Despite subtle clues that a spirit lived with us, none of us believed it until we experienced the paranormal on a visit to a famous haunted hotel.

Chapter THREE

In July 2007, my sister and her family came to Fort Collins from Washington State for a visit. The trip was routine at the start. We drove to Colorado Springs and took the train to the top of Pikes Peak, where we had just enough time to get altitude sickness and choke down some of the worst hot dogs ever consumed by humans. We toured Old Town Fort Collins and drank a few beers at the New Belgium Brewery, but the routine nature of the visit was about to change in ways none of us could have imagined.

My twenty-five-year-old niece Kimberly proposed we go on the ghost tour at the Stanley Hotel, which is famous for paranormal activity. It was here that author Stephen King stayed with his wife Tabitha one snowy evening and found the inspiration for his novel *The Shining*.

"Come on Ken," my sister Debbie said. "It will be fun."

At this point in my life, I had mixed feelings about the subject of ghosts. As a boy, I loved to read stories from C. B. Colby's book *Strangely Enough*. When I was sixteen, I watched a television program about the supernatural. In one segment, a man claimed to have left a tape recorder on a grave that recorded the voice of the person buried there. After I discussed the show with my best friend Darrin Mason, our curiosity got the better of us, so one dark night we headed out to Arlington, Texas, armed with a tape recorder.

A tall brick wall surrounded the first cemetery we came to. The place was shrouded in darkness and uninviting to a couple of kids with big imaginations. We were about to give up when I remembered that my older brother Mike used to live in an apartment located next to a graveyard. The cemetery was directly across the street and had no fence around it—the perfect spot for a couple of would-be ghost hunters to apply their trade.

We drove to the apartment building and parked. With hearts pounding, we made the short walk to the burial ground. I placed the tape recorder on a grave, pushed the record button, and we made a hasty retreat to the car. You can imagine our surprise when an Arlington police officer showed up to ask what we were doing, and you can imagine the look on his face when we explained our purpose for being there. After a quick check of our backgrounds to see if we had outstanding warrants or were escapees from a psychiatric hospital, the officer left us to our ghost hunt. I wish that I could say our experiment produced tangible results, but the recorder only picked up the sound of the whistling wind.

My interest in the supernatural waned as I grew older. I still watched an occasional horror movie, but I had no desire to hang out at graveyards in the middle of the night while trying to gather evidence of life beyond death. This is not to say I stopped believing in the possibility of ghosts. Too many credible people had reported seeing spirits for me to dismiss them. However, I had never experienced anything of a supernatural nature that would cause me to proclaim with absolute certainty that I believed in a spirit world. That was about to change.

Estes Park is a tourist magnet located high in the Rocky Mountains, approximately an hour's drive from Denver. Locals flock to Estes Park, especially during the summer, to escape the heat. Jagged gray peaks surround the town, thrusting violently toward the sky. When you enter town on East Elkhorn Avenue, you pass several stables offering trail rides. If you stay on this road, you soon find yourself surrounded by a variety of interesting gift shops. In the fall, a herd of elk roams downtown. During one of our visits, the elk were wandering through a residential neighborhood.

CHAPTER THREE

The Stanley Hotel, built by entrepreneur and inventor F. O. Stanley, sits on a hill on the north side of the town. It looms over Estes Park like a watchful sentinel. When you walk inside the hotel, it feels as though you have stepped back in time. The lobby is virtually unchanged from the time it first opened in 1909. Our tour guide arrived promptly at 11:00. The hotel lights shimmered across his bald head as he talked. You could tell that he enjoyed his job because he was enthusiastic about the subject of the hotel ghosts. He then asked how many people brought their cameras. "On most tours, at least one or two visitors capture something unusual," he said.

My brother-in-law took out his digital camera. I had not brought mine, a decision I immediately regretted.

After providing a brief history of the hotel, the guide led us into the music room. The room is bright and airy. Large glass windows offer an excellent view of the surrounding countryside. Dining tables covered with white tablecloths fill the floor space. At the back is an alcove where an old grand piano sits.

"F. O. Stanley's wife Flora loved to play the piano," the guide told us, "so he had this Steinway built for her in Philadelphia and delivered soon after the hotel opened. John Philip Sousa, famous for composing marching songs such as 'Stars and Stripes Forever,' used to come to the hotel and personally tune the piano for Flora."

My brother-in-law had retired from the Navy. During his time of service, he played in several Navy bands, so I was quite familiar with the work of Sousa.

The guide stepped close to the piano. "Numerous guests and hotel workers have heard the ghost of Flora Stanley playing at night, but whenever they approach the room, the playing stops." He placed a hand on the piano. "Would anyone like to come and sit on the bench?"

A line formed. Everyone from my family, with the exception of me, went to try out the seat. Monika tapped me on the arm. "Don't you want to sit on it?"

"You go ahead," I said. At this point of the tour, I had not experienced anything to make me believe the hotel was haunted. I am not sure what I expected to happen. The boy in me hoped that a ghost would appear, while my adult self said this was impossible.

The guide next led us to the hotel's underground tunnels. We crowded around him in the narrow passage. I noticed my sister was standing away from the group, her face pallid. I approached her. "Debbie, what's wrong?"

"I'm just feeling a little claustrophobic, you go ahead."

I rejoined the others as the guide was talking about one of the many paranormal investigations previously conducted at the hotel. "Do any of you watch the show *Ghost Hunters*?"

Hands shot up from the majority of the guests, including my sister's family. My hand stayed down. "When they filmed here," the guide explained, "the investigators heard a voice inside one of the narrow tunnels that branches off the wider main tunnel."

This news impressed most of the group and they started to whisper amongst themselves, their eyes widening. I stood in the entrance of the tunnel waiting for the voice to talk to me. When nothing happened, I sighed and left the tunnel with everyone else.

The guide has us go outside the hotel. We gathered under the window of room 217. This is supposedly one of the most haunted rooms in the Stanley Hotel and is the room where Stephen King stayed with his wife. The guide told us that many famous dignitaries had stayed in the room including several presidents. "Has anyone seen the movie *Dumb and Dumber*?"

Again, hands shot into the air.

"They filmed part of that movie here. Actor Jim Carrey checked into room 217, but on his first night, he called the front desk around 11:00 p.m. and told them to find him another room because he would not stay in 217 any longer. He never explained why he wanted to leave, but the staff believes it had something to do with the ghost of a house cleaner who haunts the room."

The guide then led us back inside the hotel for a trip up to the guest floors. You cannot access these levels unless you are staying at the hotel or on the ghost tour. Our first stop was the second floor. The atmosphere on the guest floors is dark and forbidding. The halls are narrow and filled with pockets of shadow. The woodwork and wallpaper appear straight out of the 1920s, as does the carpet. We stopped near room 217, located at the end of a short hallway. "Unfortunately," the guide said, "the room is occupied, so we won't be able to look inside."

Suddenly, the door opened and a woman peeked out. She waved for us to come over. "I saw you guys outside and thought you might like to see the room."

We crowded into the suite. It was not what I expected. It was about the same size of a room in a modern hotel, with large windows that let in a lot of light. The television miniseries based on the novel *The Shining* played on a television.

"The hotel plays both the mini-series and the movie starring Jack Nicholson on a continuous 24-hour loop," the guide explained.

After a quick tour, we set off for the fourth floor. As the group ascended the stairs leading to the fourth floor, the guide told us the history of the floor. "When the hotel opened for business, the fourth floor served as lodging for the servants and nannies, thus the rooms were smaller and hotter, since the hotel had no air conditioning. The floor is believed to be the most haunted part of the hotel."

"Let's hope so," I thought to myself.

As soon as I stepped onto the floor, a stabbing pain tore through my skull and the air became suffocating. All the energy seemed to drain out of me. The narrow hallway appeared narrower. Shadows lengthened. Trudging along with the tour group, I wondered if anyone else in our group felt the same way. The guide stopped outside room 401.

"This room had once been the nannies' lounge and was the largest on the floor."

I pressed against the door and attempted to peer inside. From what I could see, the room was slightly smaller than 217 and not furnished as well.

"There once was a young newlywed couple who spent their honeymoon in the room," the guide said. "On their first night, the bride took off her wedding ring and placed it on the nightstand beside the bed. In the morning, she was shocked to find it missing. The hotel staff conducted a thorough search without locating the ring. The couple stayed for two more nights. On the last night of their stay, the ghostly figure of a man appeared at the end of the bed. He held the bride's ring, which she promptly retrieved before the apparition vanished."

The guide pointed to the first hallway we passed. "The ghost of Lord Dunraven haunts room 407. He likes to turn the lights on and off at night or appear in one corner of the suite. He also has groped female guests and housecleaning staff."

The people on the tour turned to each other and whispered.

The guide led us to the far corridor. "I think this hallway looks the most frightening."

I looked past him to the end of the passage. Sunlight beaming through a window in the door filled the space with a warm glow, and I wondered why the guide found this spot frightening.

"Room 418," he went on, "has the highest level of recorded paranormal activity of any room in the hotel, although there are no known ghosts that haunt the room."

The group meandered down the hallway. I paused outside 418 and leaned toward the door. If there are ghosts that haunt the room, they were staying inside on this day. The guide then thanked everyone for taking the tour and left. My family gathered in the main hallway.

"That was fun," Kimberly said.

"When I stepped onto the fourth floor, I immediately had a headache," I said, "and the walls seemed to close in around me."

Monika touched a hand to her forehead. "Yeah, I got a headache too, and felt sick to my stomach."

Debbie rubbed her left temple. "I had a sharp pain on this side of my head."

I also learned that my oldest daughter Sarah suffered shortness of breath and nausea, while my nephew Tim had shortness of breath. I continued to suffer from my headache.

What was on the fourth floor that caused four healthy adults to experience similar physical symptoms at the same moment? In my mind, I had no doubt something paranormal had occurred. I could not see it, or touch it, but I knew in my heart the ghosts in the hotel did in fact exist. At this point, half of our group opted to go downstairs, leaving Sarah, Tim, and me to continue exploring the fourth floor. We walked over to room 407. As we stood outside, a strange aroma filled the air.

I gestured toward the room. "Does anyone else smell that?"

Tim sniffed the air. "It smells like burning bacon and onions."

Because the hotel restaurant was located on the far side of the building, we could not account for the source of this odor.

After wandering around on the fourth floor for several minutes, we took a small stairwell down to the third floor. When I set foot on the floor, my headache disappeared. I later consulted with the others and learned that the same thing happened to them upon leaving the fourth floor. When we left the Stanley Hotel, we went shopping in Estes Park. My brother-in-law Rick looked through the photos he had taken at the hotel on his digital camera. In one of the photos, there was a mist swirling around an open stairwell. These pictures sparked my curiosity. Would anything show up if I took photos around our home?

That night, I made a decision to take a few pictures with my digital camera before going to bed. I never imagined that I would actually capture anything unusual, after all, the Stanley is an old hotel famous for its ghosts, and we lived in a new house. Using my Sony DSC V3 camera, I snapped off approximately thirty photos in various rooms of the house. I took the pictures in low light. Most in empty rooms; however, my four-year-old daughter Amanda managed to sneak her way into a few of the pictures. When I first examined the pictures, I did not notice anything strange and quickly put the idea of ghosts out of my head.

Four nights later, August 6, at 10:00 p.m., Monika and I settled down on the couch in the family room to watch the movie *Zodiac*. We turned out all the lights in the room. Sarah was working on the computer in the front room of the house. From her position at the end of the couch, Monika could see Sarah. As the movie started, and the killer approached his first victims, Monika suddenly sat up and said, "Who's that man?"

"What man?" I said.

Monika sprang off the couch and started toward the front room. "Sarah, did you get up from the computer?"

"No," Sarah said, "I haven't moved."

Monika returned to the couch, visibly shaken.

I took her by the hand. "What did you see?"

"There was a dark shadowy figure standing in the entryway near the garage door. I thought it was Sarah, but she's still sitting in the office."

I put the movie on pause. "What did it look like?"

"I guess it was a man, all black, about 5'10", with a small head, and his arms at his sides. He must have vanished when I got off the couch."

Shadow people or shadow beings are a paranormal phenomenon that is increasing in occurrence. These supernatural creatures, known in both modern folklore and Native American religious traditions, appear as dark forms in the peripheries of people's vision and disintegrate, or move between walls, when noticed. Skeptics and mainstream science attempt to explain them away by saying they are a trick of the mind. There are many theories as to what these shadow people could be. One theory suggests that shadow beings are the shadows or essences of people who are having out-of-body experiences. Some researchers have suggested that all people travel out of their bodies while asleep and the shadow people we see are the ephemeral astral bodies of these people. Others believe that shadow people are inhabitants of a parallel dimension. According to this theory, these inhabitants have somehow found a way to intrude upon our dimension. Others speculate that shadow people may be demonic in nature due to their dark countenance and the malevolent feelings often associated with them.

As I listened to Monika explain what she had seen, I was not sure what to think. She was more open to the supernatural than I was because the paranormal is a normal part of everyday life in Indonesia. When Monika was five years old and living in the small farming community of Rangkas Bitung in West Java, her mother underwent a spirit possession.

Her mother had been feeling ill for several days. One afternoon she walked into the dining room, picked up a bowl of rice, and returned to her bedroom. There she started to eat furiously from the bowl, before rubbing rice throughout her hair and on her face. Alarmed by her mother's behavior, Monika raced to the front of the house where the family operated a store. She told her father what was happening. He immediately went to check on his wife and found her sitting on the bed in a trance-like state, covered in rice. Monika's family was Catholic, but since the majority of people living in Rangjas Bitung were Muslim, they used the Muslim holy man, known as a Kyai, for spirit possessions. Monika's father went to the town market and reported the incident to the Kyai, who returned with her father to the house.

When the Kyai saw Monika's mother, he knew that a spirit had possessed her. In Indonesia, they believe that a spirit can occupy a living person's body if that person is weak from sickness. The Kyai attempted to talk to Monika's mother, but she answered in a deep voice that was not her own. The holy man then demanded a glass of water. He blessed the water while reciting prayers from the Koran. He then took a drink of water and spit it in the face of Monika's mother. At this time, the spirit became angry and Monika's mother started to swear at the Kyai. The holy man continued to perform the ceremony, alternating prayers with the spitting of water. After about an hour of this, Monika's mother fell over on the bed and instantly snapped out of her trance. She remembered nothing of the experience.

Monika also saw a ghost when she was twenty-seven years old. She had just rented a one-bedroom apartment in Jakarta, where she lived alone. One night she had friends over for dinner. They left around 9:00 p.m. and Monika went to her bedroom to watch TV. At some point, she fell asleep. Monika woke up around 2:00 a.m. and turned off the television and the bedroom lights. She returned to the bed and lay down. Monika suddenly became aware of someone else inside the room. She glanced toward the cedar chest and saw a girl in her twenties, with long hair and wearing a purple dress. Monika could tell that the girl was a ghost by her lifeless appearance. Terrified, Monika covered her face with a pillow and whispered for the ghost to go away. After several seconds, Monika peeked out and saw that the ghost was still in the room. Burn scars covered her face. Monika again hid her face with the pillow and kept it covered until the next morning. She later learned from apartment security personnel that a train had hit and killed a young woman on the tracks that ran next to the apartments a few months prior to Monika moving in, and the spirit of the dead girl had visited other tenants.

While Monika had experienced supernatural events, I had not until our trip to the hotel. Perhaps this is the reason I doubted her report of the shadow person in our home. In addition to seeing the shadow person, Monika suffered from physical symptoms that were hard to explain. Sometimes when she sat on the end of the couch near the sliding glass door, she experienced chills that caused goosebumps to cover her arms.

Three nights after Monika spotted the shadow person, we decided to go to the Bingham Hill Cemetery. Sarah had read that the cemetery was haunted and after our experience at the hotel, we wanted to find out if the stories were true.

The Bingham Hill Cemetery in the town of LaPorte is the oldest pioneer cemetery in Larimer County, Colorado. It occupies a wind-blown spot, hidden from the road by a long narrow trail that twists alongside an irrigation ditch. Brush overgrows the trail and as you get closer to the entrance, the branches of a willow tree bow over the path to block your way. The cemetery itself is small, built on sloping, uneven ground. Yellow grass and dirt cover the cemetery grounds. Spiny cacti dot the landscape. The scattered graves dip toward the western foothills.

LaPorte rests on the northwest side of Fort Collins, snuggled in the shadows of the Rocky Mountains. The surrounding area is open and largely unspoiled with groves of hundred-year-old trees. Because we were not familiar with the area, it took us several hours to locate the cemetery, which sits approximately fifty yards off Bingham Hill Road. A small steel sign with the name of the cemetery and a trespass warning is the only clue that a graveyard is nearby. You can drive past it a hundred times without seeing it. If we had not stopped and asked for directions, we may never have found the cemetery.

Our plan was to go to Bingham Hill around midnight. Sarah, Michelle, and I would enter the cemetery while Monika waited in our van with Amanda and Rebecca. As we prepared for the trip, I started to delete the photos I had taken around our house on the night of August 2. I noticed something unusual in one of the pictures taken inside the kitchen—a white ball of light floating in the air behind Amanda. I called Monika over to the computer. "Hey, look at this picture."

She leaned over my shoulder. "What's that?"

"Well, I'm not one hundred percent certain, but I believe it's an orb."

We exchanged bewildered glances.

"When did you take that picture?"

"On the night we came back from the hotel."

"That's weird," she said before turning away.

I continued to stare at the picture as I wondered how I missed the orb before. Being a naturally curious person, I decided to take more photographs to see if anything else would appear. "Hey Michelle, come here," I shouted.

Seven-year-old Michelle trudged into the office, a sad look of resignation on her face. "What, Dad?"

"I need you to help me take some pictures."

She gazed back toward the family room. "What kind of pictures?"

I jumped up from the computer, camera in hand. "Come on, it will be fun."

Michelle sighed and fell in alongside me.

My plan was simple. Because the orb showed up inside the kitchen, I elected to take the pictures there. "Michelle, go stand near the kitchen light switch and turn it off when I tell you to."

Michelle, who was aware of the orb picture by now, approached her new job with apprehension. "Why do I have to turn off the light?"

"I want to take the picture in low light conditions."

"Why can't someone else do it?"

"Come on Michelle, it will only be for a few seconds."

Her mouth turned down as she took a position near the light switch. I stood in the entryway shooting toward the kitchen—the same position I stood at when I took the photograph on August 2. "Okay, now," I said.

Michelle flipped off the light and I snapped a picture. As soon as the flash went off, she turned the light back on. "Are we done yet?"

"No, just a few more."

She grunted.

I proceeded to take several pictures in the kitchen with Michelle present to handle the lights, and then some in the kitchen and family room without her. Back in the office, I loaded the photos onto the computer. As I examined the pictures, a twinge of nervousness fluttered inside my stomach. In the second picture I took with Michelle in the kitchen, there was a dark gray anomaly behind her, about four feet above the floor. As I zoomed in on the image, it started to change shape to reveal what appeared to be the faint outline of a person. Of the hundreds of orb photographs I would later take, this was the only one that changed shape.

"Hey guys, come in here and look at this," I shouted to my family.

Everyone crowded around the computer. Monika pointed at the screen. "What is it?"

"I don't know. I took this picture with Michelle and captured an orb. When I zoom in on it, the image changes."

To my relief, they all could see the same thing that I saw. As I continued to examine the other photographs,

I found another picture with a sphere. Michelle was not present when I took this photo. I stood in the entryway shooting into the dark kitchen and family room. The picture shows a small almost transparent orb floating over the kitchen floor, and a larger white ball of light that appears to be flying straight out of the back of the loveseat.

Prior to taking these photographs, I had no experience with orbs. None appeared in the thousands of family photographs I had taken since Sarah's birth. Paranormal researchers debate the significance of orb photographs. Everyone has an opinion on what they represent and these opinions vary wildly. Ghost hunter Troy Taylor believes the majority of orbs captured on film are not supernatural in nature, but some are paranormal. Jason Hawes and Grant Wilson, founders of The Atlantic Paranormal Society, dismiss all orbs. However, by their own admission, they made this declaration when starting their organization in order to publicize their group.

Most orbs are not visible to the naked eye, although they appear through infrared monitors and on photographic film. They are luminosities, generally round in appearance. Some people believe these anomalies are the spirits of those who have died. They suggest that spirits take the orb shape in order to move easier.

The problem with orb photography, according to some researchers, is that the spheres are easy to produce under certain conditions, especially when using a digital camera.

Since digital cameras started to become popular in the early 1990s, the number of orb photographs increased dramatically. The people who dismiss these photographs argue that the anomalies are the result of dust in the air that reflects light back into the lens of a digital camera or from lens flare caused by light reflecting off something shiny back into the camera lens. Additionally, bugs can produce these balls of light, as can certain weather conditions, especially when there is moisture in the air.

When orbs started to appear in my photographs, I was not aware of the controversy surrounding them. All I knew was something strange kept showing up in my pictures and I could not explain what they were or why they were there.

After examining the photos, we continued with our plan to visit the cemetery. Because of the pictures, I had lost much of my earlier enthusiasm. After all, why go to the cemetery to find ghosts when we may have them in our house? Around midnight, we piled in the van. Despite the late hour, no one was sleepy, but Sarah and Michelle did appear to be apprehensive. We set off for the store to obtain the supplies we needed: flashlights, bug repellent, camera batteries, film, and a walking stick to sweep the trail for rattlesnakes. It was nearly 2:00 a.m. as we sprayed ourselves with hideous smelling bug repellent. When Sarah, Michelle, and I climbed into the van, Monika immediately put down all the windows and fanned the air. Equipment in hand, we set off for Bingham Hill.

Darkness cloaked the cemetery when we arrived. Without the flashlights, you could not see more than ten feet in front of your face. I immediately sensed resistance to entering the graveyard from both Sarah and Michelle. Sarah folded her arms over her chest. "If there was a full moon out tonight it would be different."

I exited the van and walked to the cemetery gate. When I shined my flashlight down the narrow path that led to the burial grounds, a soft glow spread for a few yards. Beyond that, the darkness was ink black. "Are we going or not?"

Sarah and Michelle came alongside me. They stared down the path into the gloom and both shook their heads. With tails tucked, and smelling so bad I wanted to gag, the mighty ghost hunters made a hasty retreat.

Chapter FOUR

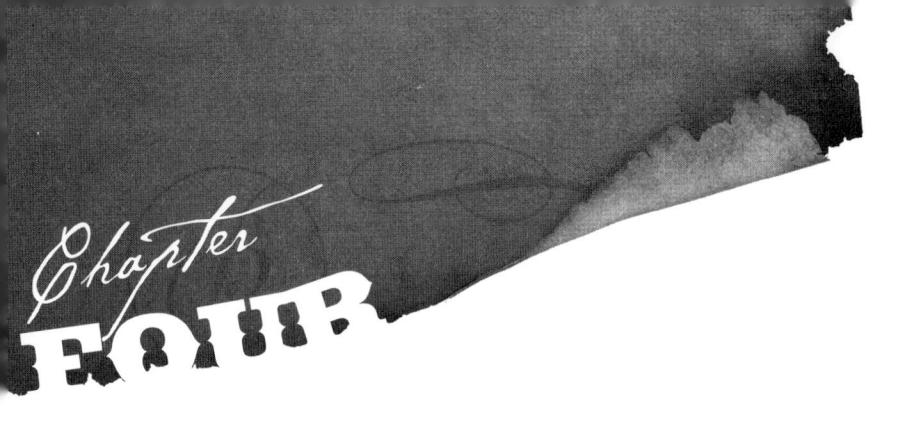

After a good night's sleep and an extra long shower, I faced the morning with renewed confidence. I managed to put the memory of our trip to Bingham Hill out of my mind. What I could not forget were the anomalies in the photographs from the previous evening. Excited by the prospect of having a ghost in the house, I called my parents. As expected, they were not as excited as I was, but after some prodding, they agreed to come over for dinner and look at the pictures.

My father is a true skeptic when it comes to ghosts, so I was not surprised when he chuckled at the photographs. "What am I supposed to be looking at?" he said in a mocking tone.

My mother, who is more open to the possibility of ghosts, conceded that the pictures looked strange. "I wouldn't want to live here with any ghost," she said.

After dinner, we settled in the family room to watch football. I wanted to continue my investigation, so from time to time; I flipped off the lights in the room and took pictures. My father voiced his displeasure with a series of low grunts.

I immediately examined the photos on the camera's viewfinder and observed white balls of light in a couple of the pictures. I then loaded the photos into the computer for a better look. In one of them, two orbs appeared above the couch where my father was sitting. The larger of the spheres was bright white with a nucleus in the form of a misty swirl or horn. I brought my parents into the office to show them these new pictures.

"Well, what do you think?"

My dad grunted. "I think you need to find something better to do with your time than chasing after ghosts."

Unfazed by my father's comments, I took more pictures after my parents left. Once again, I turned off the lights as I took photographs all around the house, the majority in the kitchen and family room. In one photograph, Monika is sitting on the couch with the kids present, but not in the picture. Behind her, coming out of the blinds above the sliding door is a greenish cloud. The cloud arches from the blinds in an L shape, with the widest point at the upper arm. I wondered if this strange cloud could be ectoplasm. Ectoplasm, identified with the formation of ghosts and hypothesized to be an enabling factor in psychokinesis, is used in levitation, transfiguration, producing raps, and communicating through trumpet mediumship. Ectoplasm, extracted from mucous membranes, escapes from the corner of eyes or mouth, and the nostrils. Mainstream science does not accept the physical existence of ectoplasm for a variety of reasons, including the fact that researchers duplicated the photographic effects said to prove the actuality of ectoplasm using non-supernatural materials.

In another photograph taken on the same night, a cluster of spheres appears above Michelle's head as she stands near the sliding door in the kitchen. When you zoom in on one of them near the top of the group, you can see a face. Could this be the result of apophenia, the experience of seeing patterns or connections in random or meaningless data? Carl Sagan hypothesized that human beings are "hard-wired" from birth to recognize the human face as a survival technique.

"Do you really think we have a ghost in the house?" Monika said.

"I'm not sure," I answered, "but my gut tells me we do."

"What does that mean?"

"Nothing will change. We've been here for three years already without any problems."

"And you believe that?"

I wanted to say, "No, everything in our lives is going to be different. How can things stay the same now that we are living with a ghost?" Instead, I said, "Before we jump to any conclusions, let me do more research. For one thing, why would we have a ghost in our house? We're the first people to live here and to our knowledge there is no history of violence or tragedy associated with the house or the surrounding land."

"Maybe the ghost followed us from the hotel," Sarah said.

"Well, I suppose that's a possibility if we do in fact have a ghost," I answered.

Of course, our lives did change immediately. Everyone came to believe the bottom floor of the house belonged to the ghost, especially at night. No one wanted to be in the family room alone after dark, which meant all of us headed to bed at the same time. For some reason, we believed the ghost stayed downstairs while we slept in the upstairs bedrooms. If I had to go downstairs at night, I developed the routine of turning on lights as I went, first at the upstairs landing, followed by the stairs, front entryway, downstairs bathroom hall light, and finally the kitchen. I did this because I was not ready for the ghost to materialize in front of me.

I found that ghosts occupied my thoughts from the time I awoke until the time I went to bed. The question of why we might have a ghost in the house stayed with me. I went to our local library and checked out every available book on the subject of ghosts as well as spending hours on the internet researching the numerous websites dealing with the paranormal. Aside from wondering why we had a ghost, I also wanted to know exactly what a ghost was. Author J. Allan Danelek describes ghosts as the disembodied energy of a deceased human being that appears not only self-aware, but also quite capable of interacting within the linear world of time and space. Accepting that ghosts are real and inhabit a plane of existence paralleling or overlapping our own, the question becomes, why do they appear to us? I learned through my research that ghosts have distinctive personality types, and these differences influence the nature of a haunting. The basic subcategories of ghostly personalities are familial, historical, and anonymous.

Familial personalities are the most common type of spirit. They represent family members or friends and typically appear soon after the person has died. A grieving spouse or parent often views familial personalities only once, as they appear in order to comfort the bereaved. My late grandmother told us she saw the spirit of her second husband not long after his death. He appeared before her in the hallway, looking as he did while alive. She attempted to communicate with him, but he vanished as she stepped toward him. Because the purpose of the familial personalities is to comfort, they are not usually associated with long-term haunting.

Historical manifestations are spirits of people not personally known to the witnesses, but are still identifiable as a recognized deceased person. A well-known example is Abraham Lincoln, whose spirit reportedly haunts the White House. However, the deceased person need not be famous to qualify as a historical manifestation; simply being identifiable to the witness is enough. These spirits can be long-term manifestations, haunting a locale for years or even decades. They usually consider themselves a part of their environment.

Anonymous manifestations are those whose identity remains unknown, without a record to identify them. These are often long-term manifestations like historical ones, and therefore can be studied. However, unlike their historical counterparts, anonymous manifestations can appear afraid and confused, so they generally are not good test subjects.

Understanding the various types of ghosts brought me no closer to learning why our house was haunted. Ghosts typically had a reason for being in a certain location. Familial personalities appear because they know the living residents. Historical manifestations stay in an area because it has special meaning for them. Why did we have a ghost? I had no family members or friends who had recently passed away. If the ghost felt connected to our house because of the location, I would need to do more research on the surrounding land before I could identify it. Was it possible a wandering spirit happened to visit us for no apparent reason?

I came to believe encounters with spirits occurred more often than reported. On several occasions when I started talking to someone about our ghost, they opened up and shared their own ghost story. A local business owner told me he thought his house was haunted because lights turned on and off by themselves and he heard strange noises. He also said one of his friends who worked as a nurse reported seeing numerous spirits at the hospital where she worked. I ran into a man at the Fort Collins Museum who told me a house he lived in on the east side of Fort Collins had three ghosts, and several members of his family saw them. When my parents lived in Silverdale, Washington, they often heard strange noises inside their house, such as footsteps on the stairs. My sister told me the piano in her home has played without anyone being in the room.

The next morning an overcast sky darkened the interior of the house. I decided to take photographs to see if anything would appear during the day. My daughter Amanda approached me as I worked. "Daddy, why are you taking pictures of the wall?"

"Daddy is wondering if the orbs will show up when the lights are on."

"You mean the ghost?"

"Yes, well, I think it's a ghost."

She rubbed her chin as she thought. "Do ghosts come out during the day?"

"I would assume so."

"Okay, Daddy, I will let you know if I see any."

Her questions revealed the prevailing mindset of everyone inside the house. During the day, the house belonged to the living, but at night, it was the realm of the ghost. Darkness brought apprehension and fear, especially for Sarah and Monika.

I took sixty photographs during the day and when I examined them, discovered white balls of light in several pictures taken inside the kitchen and family room.

That night, we went to go watch a meteor shower. Before we left, I set up my Sony handycam, which has a nightshot feature, on the kitchen table, aimed toward the sliding glass doors. Sarah held open the door that led to the garage while I started the camera and turned out the lights.

Our plan was to drive up Highway 287 toward Wyoming to get away from the city lights. The further north we traveled, the blacker everything became. We started to think about our accident with the bull in Texas the previous summer. I had recently read an article in the local newspaper discussing the high number of accidents in the area involving wild animals and livestock. Sarah, who had been driving when we hit the bull, became nervous. "Dad, I think we had better turn around."

Monika chimed in. "Yeah, I agree, it's not worth it."

We returned home, having been gone for just over an hour. Typically, when we arrived at night, Sarah would be the first one out of the van and inside the house, while Monika and I helped her sisters. On this night, Sarah remained planted in her seat. "There's no way I'm going in there first."

It was up to me to walk into the dark house and turn on the lights, something that would not have bothered me just a few days ago. Now, my heart raced as I entered the blackness as if I was stepping through the gates of Hell. A feeling of relief swept over me as my hand located the light switch.

After tucking the little girls into bed, I hurried downstairs to watch the video. I pressed my face close to the tiny flip-out screen and hit the play button. The only sound on the tape was the occasional roar of the air conditioner as it kicked on. The camera's backlight created an eerie white glow against the blinds. Several minutes passed with no activity on the tape. I was starting to feel foolish for having ever believed a ghost might live with us, and then something moved across the screen. I quickly rewound the tape to watch again. A white sphere floated in front of the blinds. My stomach twisted into knots. What appeared on the video was alive and pulsating, like a beating heart. I let out a whoop and raced to tell Monika and Sarah about my discovery. "You've got to come see this," I said and practically dragged them into the kitchen.

Monika and Sarah leaned close to the camera to watch the film. When the orb flew past, they straightened and looked back at me. I saw fear and apprehension in their expressions, not enthusiasm.

"That's great Dad," Sarah said, "now I know I should be worried."

"You have nothing to be worried about."

She started up the stairs to her room. "Yeah, right."

"Aren't you afraid?" Monika said.

"No, why should I be afraid?"

Monika shook her head. "Well, I am." She also headed upstairs. When I realized I was now alone, I hustled to round up my equipment in order to join them.

I had a hard time falling asleep. My mind kept replaying the image of the anomaly on the video. I became determined to learn as much as I could about our late night visitor. Having no experience in this kind of investigation, I knew I would need to trust my instincts and be willing to try new methods for gathering data. After reading digital cameras could produce false orbs, I made a decision to try using a 35mm camera to learn if the white balls of light still appeared. I purchased two Kodak disposable cameras that used 800-speed film and took forty photographs inside the house in both low light and normal conditions. When I had the film developed, I found spheres in six of the pictures. This meant they appeared more frequently in the photographs taken with the 35mm camera than those taken with my digital camera. I then took fifty-four photographs with the Kodak camera and they appeared in a dozen pictures.

I concluded that if we indeed had a ghost living with us, the next step would be to attempt communicating with the spirit. What happened next still sends shivers down my spine.

Chapter Five

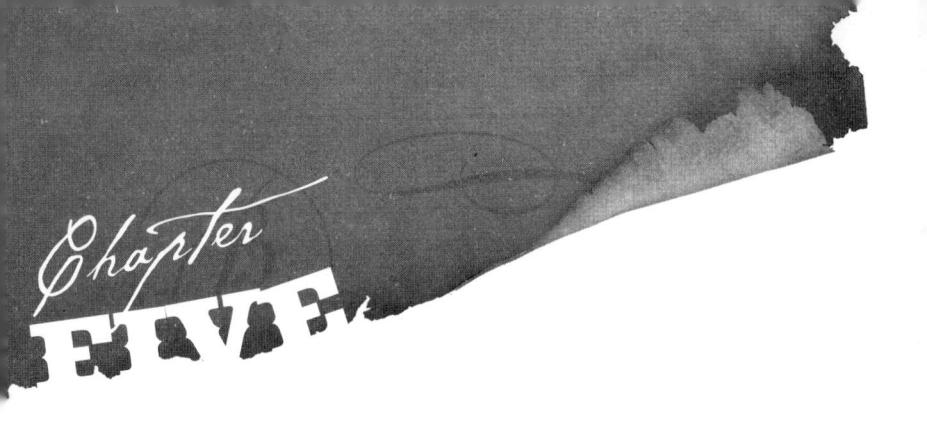

When I showed my dad the video of the anomaly floating across the screen he chuckled and said, "Well, I noticed something. What it is, I don't know."

He was right, of course. While I was convinced the orb's appearance supported the earlier photographic evidence and established we had paranormal activity inside our home, I still could not be completely certain. I needed to investigate further and so on the night of August 13, 2007, I gathered my family around the kitchen table, and we talked into the darkness, hoping for a response from an unseen visitor who was dead.

"Everyone take a seat," I instructed, "but leave me the spot at the head of the table behind the video camera."

I must admit, my adrenalin was pumping with anticipation. I felt nervous, and excited, and could not wait to get started. Others in my family did not share my enthusiasm, especially Sarah, who believed we were crossing a boundary between two worlds not meant to be crossed.

Sarah folded her arms over her chest. "Remind me again why I need to be here?"

"The whole family needs to be here," I said.

Sarah rolled her eyes and reluctantly took her spot in one of the chairs nearest the sliding door. Because I recorded the majority of activity around the door, we had come to think of the sliding door as a portal between our world and the spirit world. Monika sat across from Sarah next to Becky, with Amanda and Michelle closest to me. Becky and Amanda squirmed on their chairs like typical three- and four-year-olds. It was hard to tell if they were nervous or enthusiastic. Michelle bounced on her chair with excitement.

Once again, I aimed the video camera toward the sliding glass door. "Everyone ready?" I got up to go turn out the light. Our warm, secure world vanished in a heartbeat. Now we had entered the realm of the ghost. A hush fell over the room as I turned the camera on in nightshot mode. My heart thundered against my sternum. I started to sweat. What was I going to say to a ghost? I opened my mouth and started to speak in a deep drawn out voice, which did not seem to belong to me. "It is August 13, 2007. We are gathered here to communicate with the spirit living in our house. Present are myself, Ken Harmon, my wife Monika, and my daughters, Sarah, Michelle, Amanda, and Rebecca. Will you speak with us?"

If the ghost answered, we did not hear it, so I pressed on, asking a different question approximately every two minutes. These questions included, "What is your name? Are you a man or a woman?" And so forth. We filmed for about twenty minutes before stopping. I could have continued for much longer, but Amanda and Becky started to get sleepy, and Sarah was ready to spring out of her chair at any moment.

I rewound the tape and hurried into the office to watch. A couple of minutes into the video, a white ball of light floated through the picture. Four minutes later, I asked the question, "Did you die a long time ago?" A whispering voice answered, "Yes."

I nearly leaped out of my skin. I played it back with the camcorder speaker pressed against my ear. Upon hearing the voice again, I let out a whoop and ran into the family room. "There's a voice on the tape!"

Monika and Sarah both looked at me with wide-eyed amazement. "You're joking, right?" Sarah said.

"Come into the office and take a listen," I said.

They followed me into the office and the three of us leaned close to the camcorder, but the little girls made so much noise that we ended up on the front porch huddled close to the speaker. When the ghost voice whispered, "yes," they both pulled back.

"Did you hear the voice?"

"I heard it," Monika said.

"Me too," Sarah agreed.

This latest discovery reinforced my earlier belief that we had a ghost living with us. Of course, I wanted to tell the world about the tape. I called my sister Debbie in Washington State, and my best friend Darrin in Texas. When I played the tape for them, they both heard the voice.

"Have you considered contacting the local clergy?" Darrin said.

"Uh-no," I told him. "Do you really think I should?"

"I don't think you're supposed to be talking to ghosts."

"Who says?"

"I think it's in the Bible," Darrin said.

"Okay, I will keep that in mind."

After hanging up the phone, I started to think about what Darrin had said. As a police officer, I had looked into the face of evil, and learned that it was not always easy to recognize. Back in 1984, a young girl named Michelle Trimmier went missing from her home in the town of North Richland Hills. One night as I patrolled on the midnight shift, I received a call regarding a disturbance. When I arrived, two frightened women met me at the door of a house. One of them told me that she lived next door to the girl missing from North Richland Hills. After learning the police suspected her boyfriend John David Robertson of being involved in the girl's disappearance, she moved out of the house without telling him. Somehow, he discovered where she had gone and was now driving up and down the street in front of her friend's house. About this time, she pointed and shouted, "There he goes!" An older red pickup truck zoomed past. I ran to my patrol car and chased the truck down. Robertson seemed nervous and kept his gaze down, but at no time did I feel threatened. I had the dispatcher contact North Richland Hills detectives, but they advised to let the suspect go unless I had a legitimate reason to arrest him. I did not, so I stood and watched him drive away. A few days later, investigators discovered the girl's body buried on a property Robertson owned. After his arrest, and escape and subsequent recapture, John David Robertson committed suicide by hanging himself in his jail cell. This man represented the worst kind of evil, but you wouldn't know it just looking at him. At no time had I considered the possibility that the ghost living inside our house was evil. Should I start to worry? My gut said no, but the thought remained in the back of my mind.

At this point, I had no real plan in terms of doing a formal paranormal investigation inside our house. I opted to concentrate my filming in the kitchen and family room, focusing on the area around the sliding door. I also resolved to conduct an experiment to discover if I could produce false orbs in low light conditions using my digital camera.

Since there was no obvious connection between the ghost's appearance and our home, I wondered if spirits lived all around us, in every house and building. To test this theory while also experimenting to see if I could produce anomalies, I took numerous photographs inside my parents' house. I chose their basement because it provided low light conditions and had numerous reflective surfaces including a large wall mirror, glass tables, a large entertainment center with glass doors, and various pictures on the walls covered in glass. After I took the photographs with the camera's flash working, I checked the results. Nothing out of the ordinary appeared in any of the photographs.

When we arrived home, I tried another experiment. I went into our garage and turned out the lights. This produced near total blackout conditions. I took three photographs. As with my parents' basement, there are numerous reflective surfaces inside the garage including the windows of our van. Additionally, there is a fair amount of dust. The results from this test were the same as before: nothing strange showed up in any of the pictures.

Later that night, I gathered my family in the kitchen to attempt another communication with the ghost. Sarah stood with her arms folded across her chest at the kitchen table. From the expression on her face, I sensed she felt unease about being present.

"Okay, everyone pick a seat," I said.

Chairs screeched over the hardwood floor as everyone took their place. Sarah remained standing. "Dad, I don't want to do this."

"Come on Sarah, we need you here."

"You don't need me and I don't want to do it. I'm not comfortable with this."

"Why?" I inquired.

"I feel like we are dealing with unknown forces, unknown spirits, and energies, and I don't want to go down that road. A person doesn't touch a live electrical wire if they don't want to get shocked. I just want to go to my room."

I was disappointed, but making Sarah stay would have been a mistake. "All right, go ahead."

After Sarah left, I glanced around the table. The little girls bounced on their chairs with excitement. Monika sat straight-faced. She was not scared, but apprehensive—and who could blame her after what had occurred on the previous night.

When we finished, I reviewed the tape. One of the balls of light appeared right away. The ghost also answered my question, "Do you remember crossing over to the other side?" Twenty seconds passed and a voice whispered, "Yes, I did."

I made a couple of changes before we held our next communication. To prevent outside light from coming in, I put black cloth over the sliding glass door and the two windows on either side of the door. I also took photographs prior to starting, thinking this might signal to the ghost we were preparing to make contact.

Before I next filmed on August 16, I determined we should sit closer to the sliding glass door. I wanted us to do this for two reasons: first, so we appeared in the video, and second, to find out if we would experience any strange sensations or be able to see an orb with our eyes. We pushed back the table and arranged our chairs in a semicircle near the blinds. Despite reservations, Sarah agreed to join us. Monika, Sarah, Michelle, and I took turns asking the ghost questions for twenty-six minutes. When I reviewed the tape there was no activity on it, as if the ghost had stayed away because we invaded its space.

During this first week of my investigation, I suffered headaches that often lasted throughout the day. One morning while I reviewed a tape from the previous evening, I developed a headache that went away when I stopped watching, only to return when I played the tape again. Monika also suffered headaches.

I continued to film on a nightly basis. Sarah and Monika stopped attending the majority of the communications, and on most nights, it was Michelle and I sitting at the table. Amanda occasionally joined us. We talked with the ghost for approximately twenty minutes and left the camera running when we left to go upstairs. I waited for the tape to run out and made my way downstairs to watch the video. At first, no one wanted to stay alone downstairs, but now it did not bother me to sit by myself downstairs with the lights on.

My obsession with the investigation started to take a toll on my marriage. I decided to take a couple of days off from filming. When I resumed on August 22, I filmed inside the family room while Monika, Amanda, and I watched a movie. I wanted to see if the ghost would interact with us. I placed the video camera on the mantel over the fireplace, aimed toward us on the couch. We started the movie around 10:00 p.m. While we watched, nothing strange occurred, however, upon reviewing the video, I saw that a white ball of light appeared next to me at 10:19 p.m. and shot straight up toward the ceiling before vanishing.

At this point, the question that dogged me was, why do we have a ghost in our house? While I remained open to almost any possibility, the idea that a ghost followed us home from the Stanley Hotel seemed remote. A more likely scenario involved a ghost who had an attachment to the surrounding land. With this in mind, I began to research the history of Fort Collins.

In 1862, the U.S. Army established Camp Collins on the Cache la Poudre River in order to protect the trading post from attacks by Native Americans. A community quickly grew up around the fort, and became a center of trade, shipping, and manufacturing. The development of irrigation canals brought water to the area and farming expanded. During the 1880s, construction took place on a number of elegant homes and commercial buildings. In the latter part of the twentieth century, the city experienced a growth spurt with the arrival of several technology-based businesses.

I started to research local cemeteries and learned that several small pioneer graveyards were scattered throughout the county. Could a grave be located close to our home?

Two of the people involved in recording the location of marked graves in Larimer County were Duane and Susan Kniebes. I emailed them, and inquired if they knew of any gravesites located in southeast Fort Collins. Susan emailed back and said there were several old pioneer cemeteries in close proximity to our subdivision. Two of them were located on the old Williamson property, less than a mile east of our house. After explaining my reason for writing, Susan told me she and her husband Duane, a retired chemist and physicist, would be happy to come visit our house, and check for gravesites on our property. Susan and Duane are the Larimer County volunteers for a joint effort of the Colorado Council of Genealogical Societies (CCGS) and the U.S. Geologic Survey to locate and GPS pinpoint all of the graves and cemeteries in Colorado. Their technique in finding and/or confirming the location of graves not marked by a formal, inscribed headstone involves the use of dowsing rods. An employee at a local cemetery taught Duane how to use the dowsing rods to confirm burials. Cemetery employees use the rods to find unmarked graves in old, large family plots. (In the early days, families sometime buried individuals without notifying the cemetery officials and the cemeteries' early records are sometimes incomplete.)

According to Duane, "The technique used to dowse for graves is much like using dowsing rods—sometimes called 'witch sticks'—to find water. The L-shaped rods, which could be of any length convenient to handle, are usually fashioned from steel, about one-eighth inch in diameter. The rods are held lightly in the hands both parallel to each other and parallel to the ground. The rods are held by the bent handle, keeping the thumbs well out of the way and the fingers low enough to not interfere with the rod's movements. For most users, the two rods cross over a gravesite, seemingly on their own accord. An experienced dowser can even sometimes distinguish whether the person buried is a man or a woman depending on how the rods react."

Based on their experience finding graves, Duane and Susan have observed that remote children's graves are usually placed somewhere within easy sight of a home or in areas protected from weather, while adult graves tended to be placed at the tops of rises and hills, where the view is agreeable.

When they started the project, their original goal was to verify sixty-nine gravesites in Larimer County, including cemeteries, listed in a survey published in 1985 by the CCGS. By November of 2010, they had found all but one of the original sixty-nine gravesites, plus an additional one hundred gravesites. Was it possible they would find a grave in our yard? We would have to wait for the Kniebeses to visit to find out.

Chapter SIX

As I pressed onward with my investigation, I wanted to bridge the chasm dividing us from the spirit world. To this point my efforts to entice the ghost into appearing involved taking photographs before holding our communications, having the kids present prior to and during filming, and using a strobe light inside the kitchen. Anything that would signal our intention to make contact. Frustration set in as I struggled with the question of what I had captured on film. In my heart, I believed the anomalies represented paranormal activity, but I had no way to authenticate my findings. The level of activity remained consistent, with between one and three spheres appearing on most nights. I wondered if there was a way to further interact with the spirit world. Was it possible to introduce stimuli to produce a change in the ghost's behavior?

My first attempt at introducing stimuli took place on August 29. I had read numerous articles that said ghosts fed off electrical current created by battery-operated devices, and by doing this could manifest into human form. Paranormal investigators from around the world have reported battery life draining from their equipment as they investigated haunted locations. How does the absorption of energy allow a ghost to appear to us? Mark Macy, a prominent researcher in the field of ITC, communicating with spirits through the use of electronic devices, suggests there are many worlds of spirit, all superimposed over our physical world. Entities in those worlds sometimes interact with our world, and we attract live spirits who resonate with our disposition. If this is true, and there are numerous spirit worlds surrounding us, what separates them? According to Macy, each realm has distinct vibration waves, not like a radio or TV frequency, but rather a vibration of consciousness that makes each realm of existence unique and discrete. When a ghost absorbs electrical energy, it changes the vibration at which they move, weighing them down and making them easier to capture on film. I noticed that during previous filming sessions, my video camera suffered electrical interference. On the video, the bottom of the screen shook while the camera made a grinding noise. Was our ghost absorbing energy in order to appear to us? I wondered if I could create an electrical current to feed the ghost enough energy for it to manifest into human form.

To test this theory, I took a dozen C cell and D cell batteries and connected the positive and negative ends with copper telephone wire to create an electrical current. The batteries immediately became hot to touch, especially the D cells. I placed the batteries on plates close to the sliding glass door. I repeated this experiment for three consecutive nights without producing an increase in orb activity. Furthermore, the video captured no evidence of the ghost absorbing electricity from the batteries.

My next attempt at introducing stimuli involved recorded sound, specifically religious music. After learning that several paranormal investigators reported an increase in ghost activity following the playing of religious music, I downloaded some religious hymns onto my iPod. I had no idea what songs or artists to choose. I ended up picking four songs from the Lennon Sisters, "Eternal Life," "Old Time Religion," "Ava Maria," and "Amazing Grace." On the night of August 30, I played these songs for several minutes prior to filming. Over the course of the next hour, three orbs appeared—a number that fell within the normal activity range. I resolved to retry the experiment on the next night.

I prepared the kitchen for filming in the same manner as before with a few exceptions. To prevent the circulation of dust, I covered all the air vents downstairs, and turned off the air conditioner one hour prior to filming. After covering the windows around the sliding glass door with black cloth, I placed a flashing strobe light beneath the kitchen table and turned it on. Next, I turned on my iPod and played the Lennon Sisters for approximately one hour prior to starting our communication.

"Come here, kids," I said to my youngest daughters.

Michelle led Amanda and Rebecca into the kitchen. "What is it, Dad?"

"I want you guys to play in front of the sliding glass door for awhile."

"Oh, come on, Dad."

"The ghost seems to be attracted to you guys."

"What are we supposed to do?" Amanda said.

"Why don't you play a game the ghost might recognize, like ring around the rosy?"

They grumbled while taking their positions, before settling into a rollicking session of play that lasted for nearly thirty minutes. While they played, I took photographs around the kitchen and family room with my digital camera set on regular mode. The white balls of light appeared in multiple pictures.

"I'm capturing several orbs in photos," I told Monika. "It looks as though the ghost may be active tonight."

I turned off the strobe light when we sat down to film the communication. I asked the majority of questions.

When we finished, I turned the strobe light back on. "All right, everybody to bed," I said, lifting Amanda.

We trudged upstairs where the little girls all piled in the bed with Monika. They quickly fell asleep. I waited in the master bathroom, reading to pass the time. When I knew the tape had finished recording, I made my way back downstairs. In the family room, I sat on the couch and started to watch the video.

Anomalies appeared within the first two minutes. Another showed up two minutes later, which was a normal amount of activity on the tape. However, spheres continued to materialize at a rate of one per minute. Not only was this level of activity unprecedented, it was unlike anything I previously observed. On the earlier tapes, the orbs traveled from side to side in front of the sliding glass door. On this tape, they moved in a variety of directions, including away from the blinds. At one point, a bright ball of light exploded from the sliding glass door straight toward the camera.

I sat, stunned. Prior to this night, the highest number of anomalies that had appeared on any tape was three. Suddenly, we had fourteen in twenty-three minutes. Did playing religious music prior to filming produce this result? When only one to three of the spheres appeared, it was easier to believe they were the result of dust or insects. This unforeseen increase in activity seemed to rule out natural causes. If dust produced them, why did they disappear soon after we left the room, never to return for the remainder of the tape? I ran upstairs and woke Monika. "You've got to see this," I said, shoving the video camera in her face.

Monika groaned. "What is it?"

"Just look."

I hit the play button to start the tape. At first, Monika's expression remained the same, however, the longer the tape ran, the wider her eyes became. When the bright sphere shot toward the camera, she jumped back. "What was that?"

"There are orbs everywhere," I said.

"Because of the music?"

"That's a good bet."

She handed the camera back to me. "What does it mean?"

"I can't say for certain, but I don't think they are from dust."

"We might actually have a ghost in this house."

I laughed. "You're just now figuring that out."

The following evening I played the religious music once more prior to filming. I made a couple of changes to the experiment. I placed black 27-by-40-inch poster boards in front of the sliding glass door and the windows on either side. I also put up a dark blanket over the top half of the sliding door blinds. We filmed for twenty-five minutes and recorded a high level of activity.

The sudden increase in the number of orbs left me perplexed. Was the ghost in our house responding to the religious music? If so, this meant the spirit displayed intelligence, which opened the door for possible communication.

On September 4, a few minutes after midnight, I started to film a new video. Unlike the videos from the previous three nights, no one from the family was present during this filming. When I reviewed the tape, an anomaly materialized at the start of the film. It flew from behind the camera toward the sliding glass door before vanishing, unlike the majority of orbs that flew from the door toward the camera. This was the only orb on the hour-long tape. The decrease in activity proved disappointing after the high number of orbs I had been recording since I started to play the music.

I filmed again later in the evening of September 4, only this time with Michelle and I present. Near the end of the video, I noted more electrical interference, with the screen shaking and the camera producing a strange grinding sound.

On September 7, I filmed once more without anyone from the family present. I waited upstairs for the tape to run out and then went downstairs to watch. One anomaly showed up on the hour-long tape. It was becoming clear that a direct link existed between our presence and the activity of the ghost. To test this theory, I filmed a short communication session by myself.

You would think that someone who had confronted armed suspects, been involved in high-speed car chases, and life and death struggles with felons would not be afraid to sit alone inside their own house with the lights out. The fifteen minutes I filmed by myself proved to be one of the most nerve-racking experiences of my life. As soon as I turned out the light, it felt like I entered an alien world. My heart raced. My chest heaved. I spent the first five minutes staring straight into the darkness half-expecting something to jump out at me. I spent the remaining ten minutes with my head down and eyes closed as I asked the ghost a series of questions. When I finished, I hurried to turn on the lights. Upon reviewing the tape, I saw an anomaly in the first eight seconds. Another sphere materialized two minutes later, with a final orb flashing through the frame near the end of the film. This increase in activity supported my belief that the ghost showed up in order to interact with us.

At this point in the investigation, I wanted to capture the ghost on film while in human form. Authentic ghost photographs are rare, so I knew it would not be easy. In my research, I learned mediums often communicated with spirits telepathically. Would this work for me? I decided to try it during the next communication session. I also made a list of missing and murdered persons from Fort Collins and Larimer County and planned to use them when talking with the spirit to see if this produced a response. I knew the odds of the ghost being a crime victim were slim, but at this point, I was willing to try just about anything.

The entire family (except Sarah) took part in our next communication on September 8. I started by asking the ghost if it was one of the missing or murdered persons.

"This is creepy," Monika said as I went down the list of names.

I waited several minutes between names to give the ghost a chance to respond. After going through the list, I asked the ghost if it was David Williamson or Samuel Webster, the pioneers who had owned the surrounding property at the start of the twentieth century. I changed tactics with my next set of questions.

"If you are here with us, make your presence known by appearing or by making rapping noises."

I closed my eyes and asked the same question telepathically. Over the course of thirty-two minutes, I requested several times for the ghost to appear to us. When I reviewed the tape, I counted nine orbs during the time we were downstairs and four in the remaining twenty-eight minutes of tape with no one present.

I filmed twice on September 9. The first communication took place right after midnight. Near the end of the tape, there is a loud bang or rapping noise inside the kitchen.

"Monika, come and hear this," I said.

She joined me and together we listened to the sound. "What is that?" Monika said.

"I have no idea. We've never had a noise like that on any of the tapes. I did ask the ghost to make their presence known by rapping on something."

"So you think the ghost is answering now?"

I shrugged. "I started to communicate telepathically."

The second communication session took place later in the evening. Due to the rapping noise captured on the last tape, there was a heightened sense of anticipation as we prepared to hold the communication. I followed the pattern of asking questions aloud and then again telepathically. I concentrated on imploring the ghosts to make their presence known by rapping and to let us see them in human form. On the tape, activity started after one minute and remained steady until we left the kitchen. Six minutes after we left the kitchen to go upstairs rapping noises began. The rapping sounded more distant than on the previous tape, but occurred more frequently. This escalation in activity made me wonder if the ghost was responding to my telepathic messages. An answer would come sooner than I could have imagined.

Chapter SEVEN

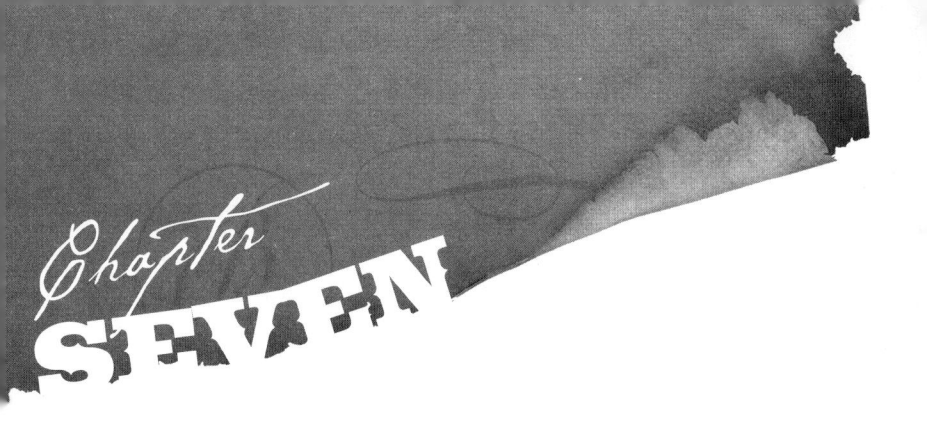

Five weeks had passed since our trip to the Stanley Hotel and based on the increasing activity inside our house, I came to believe we had a ghost living with us. Orbs appeared with greater frequency in both photographs and on video. Monika had seen the shadow person, and now we had the strange rapping noises. However, I still could not make a connection between our house and the surrounding land that would explain why our house was haunted.

My goal from the start of the investigation was to make contact with the spirit and capture it on video or in a photograph. I knew this would not be easy. People all over the world spend countless hours camped out in haunted places, cameras in hand, hoping to obtain proof that ghosts exist. Still, I had reason to be optimistic because the area of research was inside our house, which allowed me to investigate on a daily basis.

September 10 began like all the previous days. Around 9:00 p.m., I prepared the kitchen and family room for filming. Because the day fell around a new moon, the rooms were darker than normal. Monika, Amanda, and Rebecca had lost much of their enthusiasm for my work, leaving Michelle as my chief research partner. Of course, she could not do much other than keep me company, but after my previous experience filming alone, I appreciated it. The communication session lasted twenty-eight minutes. I once again requested both aloud and telepathically for the ghost to appear in human form. When I finished with the questions, I took several photographs inside the kitchen and family room with my digital camera set on nightshot. After snapping a picture, I checked the camera's LCD screen. A milky white cloud appeared over the family room television in one of the photographs. For some reason, I did not zoom in on the image. We went upstairs after I finished.

The next afternoon, I sat down to watch the video from the previous evening. Almost immediately, the camera experienced electrical interference with the familiar grinding noise and shaking. An orb appeared soon after, but this was the last activity for several minutes until the interference occurred again. After we went upstairs, several rapping sounds occurred off camera. I noticed a light flashing in the upper left-hand corner of the picture about forty-three minutes into the tape. I made note of this and finished watching. There was more activity and electrical interference toward the end of the tape.

I rewound the tape to examine the flashing light. The light appeared in the upper left of the picture, between the kitchen cupboards and the sliding glass door. It materialized from thin air, approximately five feet above the kitchen floor. The image floated rapidly in the direction of the sliding glass door, and then suddenly stopped and started to spin. It vanished during the second rotation. On closer inspection, I observed that the image was transparent, but had recognizable features. It was definitely not an orb. The surrounding darkness obscured some of the details, but the image showed a long dress without a head or arms. My initial impression was the dress dated to the late nineteenth century.

This new evidence came as something of a shock. Evidently, the ghost had responded to my telepathic requests to appear in human form. Paranormal investigators have long suspected that ghosts draw energy from electrical devices and use this energy to manifest into a shape other than an orb. Apparently, our ghost had been doing this for several days, which accounted for the electrical interference on the tapes, and would explain why she was able to manifest now.

I immediately called Monika at work to tell her about the video. "I was checking the tape from last night and I think I filmed the ghost."

"Oh really," she said in a voice that exuded doubt.

"Just wait until you get home and look at the tape."

When she arrived home, I sat her down in the kitchen with the video camera. She leaned close to the screen. Her eyes widened and then gazed up at me, the color drained from her face. "I saw her."

"I told you."

Monika examined the tape several times. "I'm not sure I believed it before, but now I do."

That evening, I sat at my computer to upload the photographs taken the previous night with my digital camera. When I came to the picture taken in the family room with the strange cloud, I zoomed in on the image. "Monika, Sarah, come here, I want you to look at this."

They joined me in the office. "What is it?" Monika said.

"Look at this picture and tell me what you see."

Sarah leaned closer and stared at the monitor screen. "It's a woman."

"Are you sure?" Monika said.

Sarah pointed to the screen and drew an outline of the image with her finger. "She's floating in the air over the television, looking toward the ceiling, her face turned to the left. Look close and you can see her right arm at her side."

I focused on the image and the woman became clear to me. "I see her. Her hair is pulled back into a bun."

Monika pointed at the screen. "Her dress is old-fashioned."

"Looks like something from the 1880s to me," I said.

"There's no doubt we have a ghost living with us," Monika said.

At this point, my entire body tingled with excitement. Of course, I wanted to tell as many people as possible. I sent emails with the ghost photograph as an attachment to my sister Debbie, my brother Mike, my parents, my best friend Darrin, and Dawn Allen from Ghost Scene Investigations, a paranormal research group based in England, whom I had contacted when the orbs first started to appear in my photographs. Everyone was able to see the woman in the picture.

Having confirmed we had a ghost, I wanted to find out more about her. Who was she? Why was she in our home? There were many questions I wanted answered, and it was frustrating not to be able to communicate directly with the spirit.

Over the next several nights, I left the camera running without anyone from my family present. Once again, the level of activity dropped off dramatically.

The entire family was present for the next communication. Once again, the ghost activity increased and remained steady the entire time we were present, and ended after we went upstairs. The strange rapping noise occurred on the tape several times after we had left. The following night I held another communication with the family present and once more, the activity level was high.

I changed the routine for the next communication. After preparing the kitchen and family room for filming, I added a second strobe light, thinking that if a barrier separated our world from the world of spirits, perhaps the light would penetrate this in order to signal our intention to visit. Another change I made was to start the tape while everyone was downstairs engaged in normal activity, rather than all gathered around the kitchen table. Michelle, Amanda, and Rebecca were in the front room office playing on the computer. Sarah and Monika sat in the family room. Monika worked on her laptop, while Sarah played her horse racing game on the TV. I turned out the kitchen and family room lights before starting the tape and aimed the camera into the family room. I filmed this way for several minutes before turning the camera toward the sliding glass door in the kitchen. Amanda and Rebecca came into the kitchen and played for a short time. When I reviewed the tape, I saw no activity while the camera filmed the family room. However, anomalies appeared in the kitchen immediately after Amanda and Rebecca finished playing there.

Did each sphere represent an individual spirit, or did they represent energy produced by a ghost? Because music or the presence of people influenced the level of activity, I started to believe that the orbs displayed intelligence. For some reason—wishful thinking perhaps—I wanted to believe the ghost only visited downstairs in our house, because that meant there was a safe, no-ghost zone for my family. But because the ghost activity typically ended after we went upstairs, I began to wonder if the ghost followed us. To test this, I placed the video camera in the master bedroom. I positioned the camera on top of the chest of drawers and aimed it toward the bed. Monika was already asleep. Rebecca was awake beside her. After starting the camera, I went into the bathroom for a couple of minutes before coming to bed. The next morning, I sat down to review the tape.

When the film starts, you see me go into the bathroom and close the door. At this point, something flashes past the camera, but it is too close to the lens for identification. Nothing happens on the tape until I come out of the bathroom and climb in bed. At this point, orbs appear. Several fly over the bed on Monika's side. The question of whether the ghost came upstairs had been answered, which explained why the orb activity stopped in the kitchen every time we went to bed. The ghost definitely wanted to be around the living.

We learned to adjust to this strange presence, the way parents adjust to the arrival of a newborn baby. After a month of communicating and gathering evidence, we no longer found the ghost threatening. It did not bother me to work downstairs alone. However, I still made a habit of turning on lights whenever I needed to get something at night. The ghost provided subtle hints to let us know of her presence. One morning as Monika walked downstairs, she heard voices as if several people were having a conversation. Thinking that the sound might be coming from Sarah's iPod, Monika looked inside her room, but found Sarah asleep and her iPod turned off. Monika continued down the stairs and again heard the voices; however, when she reached the bottom, the talking stopped. Sarah also heard mysterious conversations without locating the source. One afternoon, I was lying down on the love seat in the family room, when I heard fragments of conversation to my left. The sound crackled through the air like voices from an old-time radio program.

The ghost developed a playful nature. One night after a communication session, Michelle, Amanda, and Rebecca piled into bed with Monika and me. As we settled down for the night, it suddenly felt as if someone had lain across the lower half of my legs. I looked down to see which one of the kids had rolled onto me only to discover they were already asleep—and nowhere near my legs. On another occasion as I struggled to fall asleep, I felt someone grab one of my big toes sticking out from under the covers. One morning I lay awake on the bed with my eyes closed. I heard Monika climb out and go into the bathroom. Soon after the door closed, the clock radio on the nightstand started to make the same grinding sound as the video camera when the ghost drew energy. At the same time, it felt as if someone lifted the comforter off my left arm. I opened my eyes, thinking that Michelle had come into our room, but saw no one. Later, as I told Sarah about this, she relayed that a similar thing had happened to her the night before. She was in bed with her eyes closed when she felt the covers lifting off her legs.

After learning the ghost came upstairs, I chose to film in the kids' bedroom to see if she appeared there. I set up the video camera in their room on the night of September 18. When I turned off the light, blackness filled the room.

"Dad," Michelle wailed, "please stay with us."

"Please, Dad," Amanda said.

"Nothing is going to happen girls. I'm just filming with the video camera."

"Could you please stay with us," Amanda begged.

"All right, I'll stay for a little while."

I sank onto my knees next to Amanda's bed with my head resting on her pillow. I stayed in this position until they had all fallen asleep, and then moved to the master bedroom, leaving the video camera running. When I knew the tape had run out, I crept back into their room to retrieve the camera. As I started to watch the video, the level of activity shocked me. During the first six minutes, multiple spheres of various sizes and radiance levels appeared all around the room. Some moved slowly, others zipped past like rockets. I had never recorded this level of activity downstairs. As the kids drifted off to sleep, the number of anomalies quickly decreased. Not only did the ghost want to be with us, but she also seemed to recognize when we fell asleep, and knew to leave.

On September 20, I conducted a communication with Michelle down in the kitchen. When I watched the video, I was surprised to discover no activity. Ever since we became aware of the ghost, a part of me feared the paranormal activity inside our house would end as quickly as it started. Ten days had elapsed since I captured the ghost on film and I began to worry that whatever psychic connection I may have established with the spirit was now broken. I elected to try reconnecting with the ghost psychically in the kitchen. To do this, I wanted to hold a communication with all of the kids present.

On September 21, I prepared the kitchen in the same manner as usual. However, instead of playing religious music prior to filming, I experimented by playing children's songs from the nineteenth century. I downloaded eight songs onto my iPod and played them for an hour before we sat down to hold the communication. I also took sixty photographs in the kitchen and family room.

Despite Amanda and Rebecca making a lot of noise, I recorded a high level of anomalies, even after Amanda accidentally moved the camera and it filmed the area to the right of the sliding glass door.

Prior to filming downstairs, I placed a second video camera on top of the dresser in the master bedroom, aimed toward the bed. Activity started as soon as the lights went out in the master bedroom and remained steady until the kids began to settle down.

I tried an experiment during the next filming. Because the ghost responded to the presence of the children, I wondered if I could trick her into believing the girls were present, even if they were out of the room. To test this, I made a recording of the kids playing and singing. I gathered them in the family room around 5:30 in the evening. "I want you guys to make a tape for the ghost."

"Come on, Dad," Amanda protested, "do we have to do this?"

"Yes, Amanda, you have to do this."

Michelle grunted softly. "What should we do?"

"Should we act like dogs?" Rebecca said.

"No, Becky, why don't you guys just sing some old songs," I said.

"What kind of old songs?" Michelle said.

"You know, 'London Bridge is Falling Down,' 'Twinkle, Twinkle Little Star,' stuff like that."

After further prompting, they sang. Almost immediately, our dog Rosie began to act strange. She whimpered and paced, and would not go outside or eat. Sarah came downstairs.

"Hey Sarah," I said, "can you help me with your dog? She's acting weird."

Sarah dragged herself into the family room and plopped down on the love seat. "What do you want me to do?" She said with a sigh.

"Just put her on your lap awhile."

Sarah lifted Rosie onto her lap. Rosie continued to whimper and shake for another half-hour.

In addition to the tape of the kids, I made another playlist of songs. I researched popular songs from the nineteenth century and downloaded them onto my iPod.

I planned to start the communication around 9:00 p.m., but Monika's laptop computer stopped working, so she drove to the store to have it serviced. When she returned, we decided to watch a movie. As we watched in the darkened family room, I took several photographs with my digital camera in nightshot mode. One of the pictures had three green streaks of light moving from the outside wall near the sliding glass door toward the family room. At the end of the movie, I played the new downloaded music. I made a change in the filming routine. I started the video cameras in the master bedroom prior to holding our communication in the kitchen. I recorded nothing downstairs, but there was activity on the tape upstairs at the start. This activity resumed when we returned to the master bedroom.

I waited upstairs until I knew the tape had run out in the kitchen. I then went downstairs and changed the videotape, and started the cassette with the voices of the children singing and playing, and left it on the counter near the sliding glass door. Upon reviewing the tape, I only observed a single anomaly downstairs after I left, so the tape with the children's voices had no effect on the ghost activity.

Based on everything that had happened to this point, it was apparent our ghost displayed intelligence. She responded to my telepathic request to appear in human form. She seemed to know when we were present in a room, as well as understand that we had fallen asleep. I wondered how much intelligence she retained in the afterlife, and if there was a way to find out.

I changed the filming routine again on the next night by shooting in the kids' bedroom. The camera came on, casting a pale glow over the room.

Michelle leaned over the bed railing, a nervous look in her eyes. "Do you really think the ghost will come to our room?"

"Do you want her to?" I said.

"Sure," she answered, her voice rising.

Amanda tossed and turned on her bed. I tried to calm her, but after fifteen minutes, it was obvious she was not going to sleep anytime soon, so I let her sleep with Monika and me. After turning off the video camera, I escorted Amanda to our room. She snuggled down with her two teddy bears and quickly drifted off to sleep. I then took the video camera into the bathroom to watch the tape shot in the kids' room. What I saw astonished me. In the first thirty seconds, I counted at least fifteen orbs. They flew all around the room, the majority two feet off the ground. Some floated slowly, others streaked across the darkness. They were of various sizes and luminosity. As with the previous recordings, the spheres went away once the kids started to fall asleep. I wondered if the kids' room was the center of paranormal activity in our house. I hurried into the bedroom and woke Monika.

"I just filmed this in the kids' room and you've got to see it."

Her eyelids fluttered open and she made a face. "This had better be important."

"Take a look."

I turned on the camera and handed it to her. Her eyes widened as she watched the tape. She turned to me, her mouth agape. "Oh my God, there are so many. What does it mean?"

"I'm guessing the kids' room is the center of activity, which makes sense because the ghost has always been attracted to the kids."

"Do you think they're all right in there?"

"Sure," I said, "Ghosts can't hurt us, I don't think."

"You don't think?"

I shrugged.

On September 26, I again filmed both upstairs and downstairs. I tried something new for the video in the kids' room. I sat on the floor next to Amanda's bed and took photographs with the digital camera for fifteen minutes. To my surprise, when I reviewed the tape, I saw nothing happened in the room while I took the pictures. Did this mean the ghost knew I was taking photographs and stayed away?

The shift in activity from downstairs to upstairs left me in a quandary. Should I focus my investigation in the bedrooms where orbs routinely appeared or back in the kitchen where I had captured the ghost on video and in a photograph? If I decided to film downstairs, was there anything I could do to reestablish the psychic connection with the ghost?

Chapter EIGHT

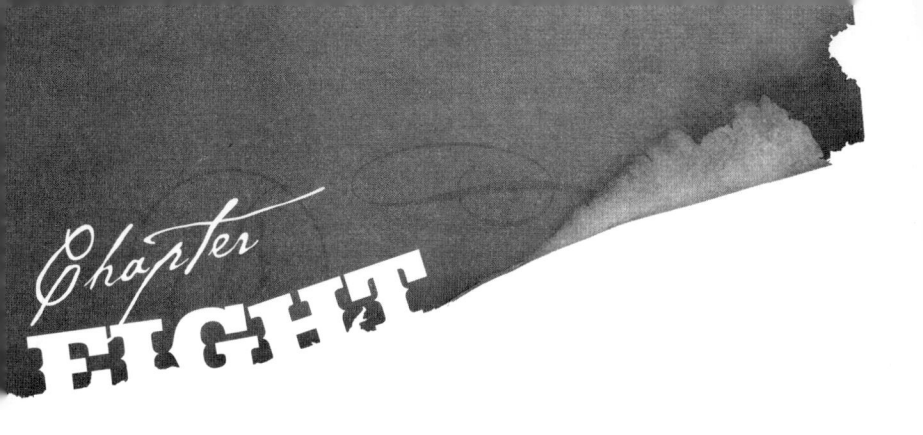

I wanted to capture the ghost on film again, and I wanted to find a way to communicate with the spirit in order to learn its identity and the reason for being in our home. To do this, I needed to reestablish a psychic connection with the ghost. I had introduced various stimuli to increase spirit activity, with mixed results. Playing religious music produced results, and the strobe lights may have had an effect. Trying to create an electromagnetic field did not produce immediate results; however, the sudden increase in ghostly activity at the end of August started about the same time I began using batteries. The number of anomalies also increased whenever I took photographs prior to holding a communication. The presence of the children seemed to produce the most activity.

My plan for reenergizing the paranormal activity downstairs involved two steps. First, I would use proven stimuli in the form of religious music and the presence of the kids. Second, I would attempt to create another magnetic field. To do this, I placed magnets on the floor in front of the sliding glass door. I chose this area because the majority of activity occurred here and because this is where I filmed the ghost in human form. In addition to the batteries, I placed a Black and Decker Power To Go battery charger on the floor. This device stores an electrical current to charge batteries in video cameras, cell phones, etc. I theorized the ghost might be able to absorb some of the energy stored inside the charger.

After preparing the kitchen for filming, I played the religious songs. To change the routine, I started the video camera in the kitchen and then had everyone go upstairs for fifteen minutes. We then crept downstairs in the dark and took positions behind the kitchen table for the communication. Rebecca and Amanda were restless, and I spent most of the time correcting them.

A single white ball of light appeared on the tape shot downstairs before our arrival. It materialized on the right side of the frame, close to the kitchen table. It floated past the table slowly and twirled, before resuming its journey toward the kitchen. I filmed again in the kids' room but fewer spheres appeared than on previous tapes, with just a few low orbs materializing near Amanda's bed.

After tucking everyone in bed, I returned downstairs and started the video camera to film a second time, only with no one present. This tape had a large amount of activity at the start, but the remaining tape had no activity. However, there was a rapping noise at several points.

I duplicated the experiment with the magnets the following evening, using thirty additional magnets. The communication started at 10:30 p.m. with Sarah, Michelle, and I present. I provided the majority of questions, but Sarah asked a couple, which surprised me given her previous resistance to anything that dealt with the ghost. Michelle fell asleep before we finished, so I ended up carrying her to the kids' room. Michelle's bed was unmade, so I placed her next to Rebecca. I then sat on the floor near the door with the video camera aimed toward the kids. In the first minute of tape, there were a high number of anomalies around Rebecca's bed.

When I worked for the police department, I learned how to respond to each type of call. For example, if we responded to a report of a burglar inside a building, the officer with the sheet followed established rules. First, he coordinated the position of his assisting officers to ensure they had the building surrounded. Next, he would call for a K-9 officer, to help search the building. Even the manner in which we searched the building was governed by rules. These rules increased the officer's odds for success and survival. I tried to establish similar rules for my investigation of the paranormal activity inside our house, knowing this was the only way I could accomplish my goal of recording the ghost on film.

As the investigation wound into October, I had reason to be optimistic about capturing the ghost on film again. During the communication sessions, I once more reached out to the ghost using telepathy and requested that she appear in human form. On October 6, I took photographs of the living room with the lights out and the camera set on nightshot. In a picture taken at 1:40 a.m., you can see the bookcases, and everything appears normal. In another picture taken one minute later of the same spot, the lower part of a woman's dress appears, floating in the air. The majority of the dress blends into the bookcase and is not visible. The dress is old-fashioned, as if from the late nineteenth century, and is solid and not transparent. I wished I had been able to capture the image sooner when the entire ghost was present, but this latest development was exciting and made me more determined than ever to collect further evidence. Unfortunately, I soon suffered a setback.

On October 9, I injured my back. I attempted to treat the injury with rest, but the pain became so intense, I called my doctor for medicine. I ended up flat on my back for almost three weeks. To make matters worse, I developed a severe case of bronchitis that required two trips to urgent care and two rounds of antibiotics.

During this time, my investigation slowed to a crawl. We held no communications, although I did film a few nights in the kitchen without recording anything.

On October 23, my back felt well enough for me to take part in a communication. We only stayed for a short time before taking the kids up to their room. I then filmed a few minutes in the kids' bedroom. I reviewed the tape after the girls fell asleep. To my surprise, there was ghost activity on both parts of the tape.

We held another communication the following evening. Again, Rebecca and Amanda made a lot of noise. I filmed in the kitchen for eleven minutes before we moved upstairs, where I filmed in the kids' room until they fell asleep. Twenty-nine orbs appeared during the short time we were downstairs. This was the most activity I had ever recorded in this part of the house. In the kids' room, orbs filled the screen like a meteor shower.

I opted to try an experiment during the next communication. I purchased a hollow wood box and planned to ask the ghost to respond to my knocking on the box. I placed the box on a small table close to the sliding glass door. I was concerned that placing the box in this location might adversely affect the level of spirit activity. In the past, whenever I placed anything close to the door, there was little or no activity. After filming for a few minutes, I stepped out from behind the table and stood near the box. I beseeched the ghost to communicate with us by knocking on the box and then demonstrated what I wanted by knocking. Unfortunately, the ghost did not attempt to communicate by knocking.

I repeated this experiment for three consecutive nights without the ghost responding. This was about to change. On October 29, Sarah and I went to my parents' house to help them put up Halloween decorations. When we returned home at 6:00 p.m., I took a shower. After finishing, I walked across the dark master bedroom toward the closed bedroom door. When I reached the door, I heard a single loud knock. I opened the door and spotted Monika walking toward the laundry room with her arms full of clothes.

"Did you just knock on the door?"

"No," she said, "but I heard a knock."

"Then it was the ghost."

Her eyes got big. "Really?"

"She must be trying to respond to my requests for her to knock."

The next night around 9:00 p.m., everyone was downstairs except for Michelle who was in the master bedroom watching television. Monika started up the stairs to check on Michelle. As she neared the landing, Monika saw a small figure wearing a white dress travel from the direction of the master bedroom into the kids' room. The figure moved quickly as if floating on air. At first, Monika thought it might have been Michelle. She went to the kids' room and found it dark and unoccupied. Monika then walked into the master bedroom where she confronted Michelle coming out of the bathroom.

"Did you just go into your bedroom?"

"No, I was brushing my teeth," Michelle answered.

I was in the kitchen when Monika rushed downstairs to tell me what she had seen.

"I think I just saw the ghost."

"What?"

She then explained what had happened and held up an arm. "Look at my arm."

Goosebumps covered her arms.

"Oh my gosh," she said fanning herself, "my heart is beating so fast."

After this incident, I was optimistic something would happen during our communication that night; however, I recorded no activity.

Many paranormal researchers believe ghosts can manifest easier on Halloween because the boundary between the spirit world and the natural world is at its thinnest point. When we returned from trick-or-treating, I immediately prepared the house for a communication, hoping to test this theory. Unfortunately, our ghost did not appear in human form, however, multiple orbs materialized, only to stop once we all went upstairs.

Over the next several days, I tried several experiments. On two occasions, I filmed in the kitchen with the little girls out in front of the camera, and both times, I recorded activity, and because Monika had seen the ghost moving in the hallway upstairs, I set up a camera on the landing to film after we went to bed. On the first night, the camera recorded no activity, but several anomalies appeared on the next night. Several spheres materialized on the third night of filming. They were smaller than what I had previously filmed and shot across the screen at a high rate of speed.

Having successfully captured and documented the ghost in the form of orbs, a full manifestation on video, and in photographs, I resolved to move the investigation in another direction. I wanted to learn the identity of the ghost and understand why she was in our house. Based on the ghost's dress and hairstyle, I theorized she died between 1880 and 1900. Because our house was new and never occupied, the ghost probably had an attachment to the land surrounding the house, rather than the house itself.

I planned to research the history of the land to see if I could make a connection between it and our ghost. With luck, we would soon know the identity of the ghost and understand why this unworldly presence visited.

Chapter NINE

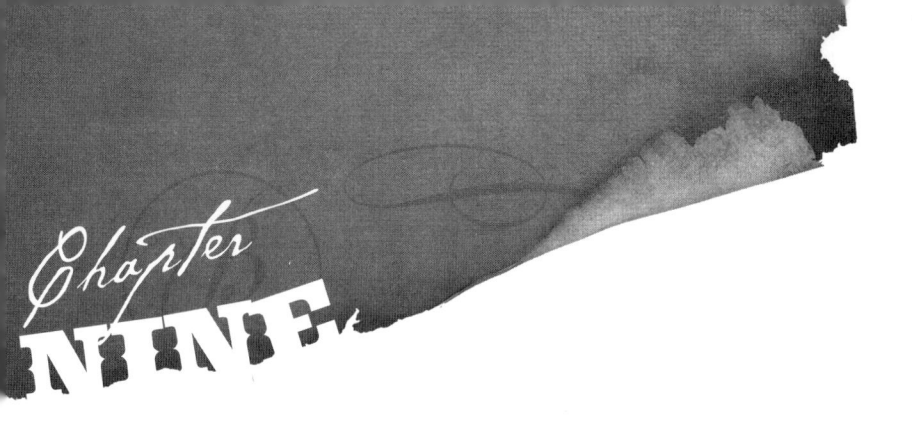

I wanted to learn the identity of our ghost, but did not know where to start. There seemed to be three possible explanations for why we had a ghost in our house: we attracted a wandering spirit, a ghost from the Stanley Hotel followed us home, or a ghost haunted our home because of a connection to the surrounding land.

I quickly determined it would be virtually impossible to learn the identity of a wandering spirit. Based on the photographic evidence, I concluded our ghost was from the later part of the nineteenth century. I could research the deaths of all women in Fort Collins during that time, but this could involve hundreds of women. I could attempt to narrow the search to women who had died tragically or from sudden illness, but this still would not explain why the ghost was in our house. Additionally, this would not take into account any women who may have died while traveling west.

Could the ghost have come from the hotel? Several ghosts haunt the hotel, but the hotel did not open until 1909, so none of them would be from the correct period.

I emailed the Stanley Hotel in October 2007 asking for the name and contact information of the general manager. They promptly emailed back with the information. Because the hotel capitalized on its reputation of being haunted, I anticipated a favorable response. So I sent the general manager an email explaining what had happened during our ghost tour at the hotel, and the subsequent events at our house—and even included the photograph that I took of the ghost floating over the TV. I told the general manager that I suspected the ghost might have come from the hotel. I inquired if a nanny or maid had died at the hotel. I also asked if I could come out to the hotel in order to take photographs on the fourth floor and I was offering to give them publicity. To my surprise, the general manager never responded to my email.

When we visited the hotel back in July, my father purchased two books in the hotel gift shop: *Ghost Stories of the Estes Valley*, Volumes 1 and 2. The books contain ghost stories told to the author by residents of the valley—including stories that take place inside the hotel. I located an email address for the author through Front Range Community College. I emailed her on November 17, explaining what was happening in our house, and asked if she had any information regarding the nannies and maids at the hotel. The author replied and said that she had heard stories about a maid or nanny dying at the hotel, however, she could not verify this. Subsequent research did not turn up information regarding the death of a maid or nanny at the hotel. Because of this finding, I concluded our ghost did not come from the hotel.

I had previously researched the historical archive pages of the Fort Collins Public Library's website to see who may have owned the land where our subdivision is now located. Based on the Great Western Sugar Company Map of 1900 (sugar beet farming was a driving economic force), I concluded that one of three men, George P. Avery, Dominick Gill, or Samuel Webster had owned the property in 1900. I knew from Susan Kniebes' research notes that David Williamson's farm had been located due east of our location. David Williamson came into the area alone in 1882 at the age of seventeen and began farming in the Harmony District. In December of 1895, he married Minnie May Webster, the youngest child of Stewart Webster. They had one child, a son named Leslie. David Williamson died in 1929 and Minnie Williamson died in 1971 at the age of ninety-five. There was nothing in their personal history connecting them to our land except that Minnie Williamson's father, Stewart Webster, was also the father of Samuel Webster.

An interesting fact about the Williamson place is that on April 25, 2001, following clues provided in historical records, Susan and Duane Kniebes discovered three burials in a small cemetery located in the northeast corner of what was left of the Leslie Williamson's tree claim (extra land that homesteaders had rights to if they planted trees on it) and another five-person cemetery that is currently located in the front yard of one of the homes of the West Chase Subdivision. (In April 2001, this second cemetery was in a field surrounded by ten metal "T" posts.) Based on Duane Kniebes' use of dowsing rods, the cemetery on the Williamson's tree claim contained one adult and two infant burials. Two rose bushes are associated with the adult grave, and one rose bush is associated with each of the infant burials. However, these graves do not belong to the Williamson family. Who were the people buried in these graves? One clue may come from information gathered during Cecilia Damschroder's interview with Charles Webster in June 1995. Cecilia, former president of the Larimer County Genealogical Society, reported to the Kniebeses that Webster told her that two people from a passing wagon train died during a flu epidemic and were buried in the northeast corner of the Williamson's tree claim and one was buried on the northeast corner of George Kechter's homestead. Duane and Susan Kniebes searched that part of the Kechter property without finding any graves, but as mentioned above, they did find three graves in the northeast corner of the Williamson property. Susan Kniebes told me there were probably many unmarked graves of pioneers scattered around Larimer County. Could our ghost have been some unknown pioneer heading west who succumbed to disease or injury and ended up buried on our land?

Another possibility, however remote, is that our subdivision had belonged to one of the Native American tribes that lived in the area before the pioneers' arrival. I found a historical account of Native Americans surprising Stewart Webster's wife Margaret as they roamed around the Webster homestead. Had the Arapaho, Cheyenne, or Sioux once used the land for a burial ground? Based on the photograph I had taken of our ghost back on September 10, I believed she was either Caucasian or Hispanic. Since the Hispanic population was practically nonexistent in Fort Collins during the 1880s, the ghost was most likely Caucasian.

Needing help researching the land, I contacted the Fort Collins Museum, which has always been at the forefront of the city's efforts to preserve its history. Originally, the building was the Fort Collins Public Library. The museum first opened in 1941 as the Pioneer Museum and moved into its present location in 1976. Shaded by century-old trees, the museum is a wonderful place to spend an afternoon. In the courtyard on the south side of the building are three log cabins, including the Janis

Cabin, thought to be the first permanent residential structure in Larimer County.

I sent the museum an email explaining we had a ghost in our house and that based on the Great Western Sugar Map of 1900, our subdivision had belonged to either Dominick Gill, Samuel F. Webster, or George P. Avery. Pat Walker, a research assistant at the museum, contacted me. Pat suggested I go to the Larimer County Recorder's Office to obtain the legal description of our land. She said with this information I could check the Grantor/Grantee indexes and deeds to trace the ownership. Unfortunately, my research hit a dead end here.

In the 1880s, the Harmony District consisted of farms located about seven miles southeast of Fort Collins. A few dirt roads connected the town with the district. Because the area remained undeveloped until the 1990s, the museum did not have a great deal of information for the Harmony District, such as tax assessor records.

On November 8, I traveled to the museum to meet Pat, who was going to assist with my research. I met Pat in the archive room. I immediately liked Pat, who is just the kind of person who should be working in a history museum. She obviously had great enthusiasm for her work and was very interested to learn about our ghost. When I emailed Pat earlier, I had attached the ghost photograph I took on September 10. When she saw the picture, Pat also thought the ghost was from the 1880s.

I brought both my video camera and digital camera to the museum. I sat down at a table with Pat and showed her some of the video I'd taken around the house. When we finished watching, Pat produced files that contained information on George P. Avery and the Webster family. Pat had already done some preliminary research on the names I provided. She told me that according to the records on Dominick Quinn, he owned farmland in the Harmony District, but never lived on it. I started to dig through the file on George P. Avery, which indicated he came to Fort Collins in 1896, and worked as a reverend. He lived in town at 504 LaPorte Avenue. His first wife, Ruth Etta Baker, died on September 16, 1900. He later remarried. He fathered several children, all of whom lived into adulthood. I wondered if Ruth Etta Baker could be our ghost, but quickly determined that she was a poor candidate. The only thing connecting George P. Avery to our land was the 1900 Great Western Sugar Map. There was no record of him ever farming, although I did find records of church members donating land to him. George P. Avery never lived on the land where our house now sits and no records linked him to anyone who lived in the Harmony District.

I turned my attention to the Webster family. According to the family history, Stewart Webster was born on October 24, 1843, in New York State. He left home at the age of nineteen to seek adventure on the

Western frontier. Stewart reached Denver, where he took a job hauling freight to the mining towns of Central City and Black Hawk. He returned east in 1864, settling in Iowa. On March 3, 1864, near Palmyra, Iowa, he married Margaret C. Fetters. Margaret was born on February 1, 1843, in Cleveland, Ohio. She grew up and was educated in Iowa. The family welcomed three children in Iowa: a daughter Mary Bell born on January 18, 1864, and sons, Henry G. born March 20, 1867, and Ruben Johnson born March 9, 1869. Another son, Samuel, was born in Cass County, Missouri, on March 12, 1871. The family moved from Missouri to Colorado in 1875, settling in Fort Collins. For a time the family lived in town on the corner of Magnolia and Smith, where daughter Minnie May was born on February 10, 1876. Stewart Webster took up the job of freighting again for a while before settling a homestead in the Harmony District around 1880, where two more sons were born, William Harrison on May 14, 1880, and David on November 16, 1886. The family lived on the homestead for approximately twenty-five years, before Stewart Webster moved back into town. During their time on the homestead, they first lived in a dugout before building a small house.

Nothing about the Websters' family history stood out in relation to our situation, until I read about their oldest child Mary Bell. Mary Bell Webster lived with her parents until she married a man named Charles Q.

Wilson on October 18, 1883. The couple then moved on to land they were leasing. Mary Bell gave birth to a daughter Leona on July 15, 1884. At this point, the Wilsons enjoyed a routine life; however, that changed in 1886. On June 2, 1886, three strangers attacked Charles Wilson and burned down their barn. According to an article from the *Fort Collins Courier* newspaper from June 3, 1886, the Wilsons lived a half mile from Stewart Webster on land they leased from William Harding.

A few months later in November of 1886, Mary Bell Wilson, her father Stewart Webster, and an unidentified male sibling came down with typhoid fever. They took Mary Bell to her parents' home for treatment. According to an article from the *Fort Collins Courier* dated November 18, 1886, a Dr. Galloway reported he was treating three members of Stewart Webster's family for typhoid fever, including Mr. Webster, Mrs. Wilson, a married daughter, and a young man. Dr. Galloway went on to say they were slowly improving and he hoped to have them all up very soon. This prognosis proved correct for Stewart Webster and the unidentified young man, but Mary Bell was not as fortunate. Ten days later, on the evening of November 28, 1886, she died at her parents' home.

In the final stages of typhoid fever, the patient becomes delirious, so Mary Bell probably was not aware of her impending death. I cannot imagine the chaos that must have been taking place inside the Webster home at that time. As Stewart Webster and one of his sons battled to overcome typhoid fever, and Mary Bell lay dying, Stewart's wife Margaret was taking care of a newborn son, David, born on November 16. This is the obituary for Mary Bell Wilson as written in the *Fort Collins Courier* on December 2, 1886.

> *Mrs. Mary B. Wilson, wife of Charles Q. Wilson, died Sunday evening, November 28, 1886, at the home of her parents, Mr. and Mrs. Stewart Webster, of a complication of diseases. Mrs. Wilson was only twenty-two years old. She was an exemplary woman in all the relations of life, and her early death has brought sadness to many hearts. She leaves a devoted husband and one child, aged sixteen months, whom she fondly cherished, to mourn their irreparable loss. Her remains were buried Tuesday, the funeral taking place at her childhood home, Rev. J. A. Long officiating. A large concourse of neighbors and sympathizing friends followed the mournful cortege to the grave.*

As I read the obituary, it struck me that I may have identified our ghost. The pieces seemed to fit. She died in the 1880s at a young age while settling into a life of her own, leaving behind a child she adored. Mary Bell Wilson fit the classic profile of a ghost; someone who died before his or her time and had a reason to remain earth bound rather than cross over. In this case, her reason for remaining seemed to be her child Leona. The ghost inside our house had always been attracted to the children, especially our youngest daughters Rebecca and Amanda. Back in August when we first noticed the strange events in our house, Rebecca was two and a half years old, and Amanda a year older, making them both close in age to Leona Wilson at the time of Mary Bell's death.

In order to make the connection between Mary Bell Wilson and our haunting, I needed to find out why she would be in our house. To do this, I needed to confirm that the Websters had lived on the land where our house sits. If I could not place the Websters on our land, the case for Mary Bell being our ghost would be weakened. In her book, *A History of Fort Collins,* historian Arlene Briggs Ahlbrandt lists the location of Stewart Webster's homestead as just west of David Williamson's farm, and if this was true, then the Websters' homestead had to be close to our subdivision, as the Williamson farm was due east of us. Additionally, because David Williamson married Mary Bell's younger sister Minnie Webster, it made sense that the families lived in close proximity.

I contacted Robert Larson, president of the Larimer County Genealogical Society for assistance. Mr. Larson put me in touch with the organization's local researcher, Carol Stetser. Carol suggested I go to the Bureau of Land Management's website and do a land patent search for

Stewart Webster. I found a land patent for Stewart Webster dated, July 12, 1889. The patent was for a homestead with the following coordinates: Aliquot Parts SE, Sec., / Block 8, Township 6-N, Range 68-W, Meridian 6th PM, State CO, Counties Larimer.

Armed with this new information, I started to examine old maps to cross-reference the land coordinates. I located an old 1899 Larimer County land plat map in the Fort Collins Library collection. The map, marked in grids, contained the information I needed. After locating Section 8, Township 6-N, Range 68-W, I cross-referenced that location against the 1900 Great Western Sugar Map. According to the 1899 Larimer County map, Section 8, Township 6-N, Range 68-W was located almost due north of Boyd Lake. On the 1900 Great Western Sugar Map, this section belongs to Stewart Webster's son Samuel and our subdivision is located in this section. This meant that Mary Bell Wilson would have lived and died here—and it made sense that the land was listed under Samuel Webster because according to the Webster family history, between 1886 and 1905, Stewart Webster developed a drinking problem. He sold his land holdings to son Samuel prior to moving back into town.

Although the information from the 1899 land patent corresponded with the 1899 Larimer County and 1900 Great Western Sugar maps, I wanted further confirmation that Mary Bell Wilson once lived on our subdivision. On the 1900 map, Samuel Webster owned several parcels of land, some of which were south, north, and east of our location. While none of these was Stewart Webster's original homestead, I wondered if the family had moved to one of these parcels at some point prior to Mary Bell's death. The best clue I had as to where Mary Bell lived at the time of her death was from the June 3, 1886, article in the *Fort Collins Courier* that described the attack on the Wilson farm. The article said the couple was leasing from William Harding land that was a half mile from Stewart Webster's home. After the attack, Charles took Mary Bell and their daughter Leona to her parents' house. I checked the 1900 Great Western Sugar Map and found a parcel of land belonging to a Willard Harding, but nothing under William Harding. The land belonging to Willard Harding was located approximately one mile east and two miles north of our house. Additionally, none of the parcels that surrounded Willard Harding's land belonged to the Webster family. Although my research about William Harding came up empty, I did locate history for a Willard Harding, who was one of the earliest pioneers in Fort Collins. However, Willard Harding never married and had no children. Could the name in the news article have been misspelled? According to both Pat Walker from the Fort Collins Museum and Carol Stetser of the Larimer

County Genealogical Society, newspapers in the 1880s often were filled with typos.

Carol Stetser suggested I go back to the Bureau of Land Management's website and try another search. She said if I entered the coordinates from Stewart Webster's 1899 land patent, it would list everyone who lived in close proximity. I did this and found that Willard Harding owned land in Section 12, Township 6 N, in range 68-W. I checked this information against the grid on the 1899 Larimer County map and discovered that Willard Harding's land was approximately one-half mile west of Stewart Webster's homestead. At last I had solid proof that not only was Stewart Webster's homestead located where our subdivision now sits, he also lived on it, and his daughter Mary Bell Wilson lived with her husband Charles Q. Wilson on land just west of Stewart Webster's house. This also meant Mary Bell died in the Webster home, built somewhere near our house.

I think it safe to assume that Mary Bell's ghost started haunting her parents' house at the time of her death. Not only had she lived and died there, her parents raised Leona, which gave Mary Bell's spirit another reason to be inside their house. I wondered if the Websters experienced the same things we had. Did Mary Bell's ghost attempt to communicate with them? Did she rap on doors or tickle their feet as they slept? Without the benefit of modern photographic equipment, they could not have seen her ghost unless she manifested before them. Had Mary Bell done this and was this the reason Stewart Webster turned to the bottle? Did the family move into town in 1905 to escape from Mary Bell's ghost?

The week leading up to my visit to the Fort Collins Museum, I experienced something unlike anything else. Every night after I fell asleep, I had the sensation of being awake inside the master bedroom. I could see the room clearly and recognized that it was night. Everything appeared normal, except I sensed a presence in the room to my left, near the bedroom door. They stood in the shadows making identification impossible, but I knew they were there and wanted to communicate with me. In the morning, it felt as if I had not slept at all. I was exhausted. I experienced this for five consecutive nights, but on the night I came home from the museum and told my family about Mary Bell, I had a deep, uneventful sleep.

The day after I visited the museum, we drove to the Harmony Cemetery, located off Harmony Road, one of Fort Collins' busiest thoroughfares. The cemetery, which opened in 1881, is small, with approximately fifty graves, and surrounded by a thigh-high brick wall. During the three years we had lived in Fort Collins, I never saw anyone visiting Harmony Cemetery. Our purpose for going was to locate the grave of Mary Bell Wilson.

We arrived at 3:30 p.m. Long shadows stretched across the cemetery ground and a whispering breeze chilled the air. The entrance is located on the southeast corner, marked by a waist-high iron gate detached from the broken wall. Sarah, Michelle, and Amanda accompanied me into the graveyard. Sarah and I moved in silent reverence, stopping to read the epitaphs not worn away. Michelle and Amanda bounded across the hallowed ground, laughing as they danced around the headstones.

It took ten minutes to locate the Webster family headstone. In front of the large stone was the grave marker for Mary Bell's mother, Margaret Webster. There were three small brown stones weathered beyond recognition on the south side of the family plot. Behind the large family stone was a diminutive white stone, approximately twelve inches high that leaned toward the earth. Carved on the stone were the initials M.B.W. The soil around the stone was so loose; I could have easily lifted it out of the ground. Behind this stone, approximately five feet away, was a larger headstone, four feet tall, the bottom shaped like a pedestal, with an urn design on top. The top section has cracked and will break off and crumble to the grass at some point. The epitaph read:

MARY B.
WIFE OF C.Q. WILSON
DIED NOV 28, 1886
AGED 21 YEARS
10 M'S, 10 D'S

As I stood in front of the stone, it felt like I belonged there, as if I was nearing the end of a long quest. It was strange to think what remained of Mary Bell's body lay before me and yet she may live inside our house. While walking around the Webster family plot I searched for the grave of Mary Bell's brother Ruben Webster. Ruben Johnson Webster was born on March 9, 1869, in Warren County, Iowa. According to family history, he died at either age ten or twelve and was buried in Harmony Cemetery, but I could not confirm this information. According to Cecilia Damschroder, former president of the Larimer County Genealogical Society and foremost expert on the Harmony Cemetery, there are two children's graves at the Webster plot, one belonging to Ruben. However, she did not know if he was buried somewhere else first and later moved. If he died in 1879, prior to the cemetery opening in 1891, his family probably buried him on the Webster family homestead.

I often wondered if more than one spirit visited our house. If each orb represented an individual soul, we definitely had more than one ghost inside the house. On several occasions, I captured multiple orbs on video. In addition, some of the orbs appeared different. Some were large, dim, and slow moving while others were larger and brighter—exploding across the room at a high rate of speed. Still others were small white circles that shot through the air, sometimes twirling before they vanished.

I never located a gravestone for Ruben Webster at the Harmony Cemetery and while it seemed plausible that he could be haunting our house along with Mary Bell, I had no evidence to support this.

While I did field research, I continued to film around the house and take photographs. Due to our schedules, we were limited in the number of communications we could hold. However, we did hold a couple of communications soon after I learned about Mary Bell Wilson. Unlike our previous communications, we now used Mary Bell's name while addressing the ghost. When I turned on the camera, orbs immediately flashed in front of the camera. Monika went into the bathroom when we first started to film. During the time she was away, we experienced a high level of orb activity. When she returned eight minutes later, the orbs stopped and did not return for the remaining ten minutes we filmed, until we stood to leave and two flashed across the screen.

After Monika observed the ghost on October 30, I again made upstairs the focus of my investigation. My routine involved filming in the kids' room and then moving the camera to the hallway between their room and the master bedroom. The ghost seemed to understand what I was doing because the orb activity shifted from the kids' room into the hallway. Sometimes the orbs floated out of the kids' room and other times they materialized in the hallway and moved into their room.

It was at this time I tried filming in Sarah's room to see if orbs would appear. Sarah did not want me to film in her room.

"Don't you want to know if Mary Bell is active in your room?"

"No, Dad."

"Why not?"

"I just don't want to know if there are orbs, okay."

I suppose it brought her peace of mind to believe that the ghost left her alone. One night I filmed briefly in her room while Sarah slept. I pushed open her door and filmed for several minutes without recording any activity. I guess parents are not the only ones afraid to go in a teenager's room.

On November 15, we filmed a communication downstairs and recorded several orbs. We then moved upstairs where I filmed in the kids' room. Once again, numerous orbs appeared until the kids fell asleep. I decided to go back downstairs alone and set up the camera in the kitchen to make another tape. When I first started filming back in August, I thought the room needed to be dark to ensure spirit activity. Over time, I came to realize that the ghost would appear even if I kept a light on in the office. This not only improved the picture quality of the videos, it also made the room feel less threatening.

As I walked into the kitchen to prepare the camera, I did so without a sense of trepidation. I think it helped that I may have identified our ghost. It was comforting to know that the spirit belonged to a young woman who by all accounts was a Christian and loving mother. After starting the tape, I remained downstairs for five minutes to hold a brief communication. Three orbs materialized on the film during this time.

That night I had difficultly sleeping. For the first time since my trip to the Fort Collins Museum, it felt as if a presence was in the bedroom, only this time there was more than one and they were not trying to communicate with me. Instead, they seemed to be up to mischief. Around 4:30 in the morning, it felt as if someone was bouncing on the end of the bed.

On November 16, I did not go to bed until after 1 a.m. Amanda was also restless after taking a late nap and stayed up with me. When I finally trudged upstairs with Amanda, I filmed in the kids' room while waiting for her to fall asleep. As usual, a number of anomalies appeared on the video until she started to drift off, at which time the activity stopped. I moved into the master bedroom where Monika was asleep. I set up the video camera on the nightstand and aimed it out into the room toward the door. I had tried to film from this position on several occasions without success, and had never recorded orbs in the master bedroom without at least one of the kids present, so I had no real expectations. In addition, I tilted the camera upward to film closer to the ceiling and most orbs seemed to move about three to four feet off the ground. The next morning when I watched the tape, I saw a sphere pass by as soon as I climbed in bed. Over the next ten minutes, there were four more orbs.

I once again felt that there were multiple presences in the master bedroom that night. Around 4 a.m., I felt the covers pulled at the end of the bed, followed by the sensation of someone pushing down on the mattress to make it bounce.

Over the next several nights, I continued to film in the kids' room and master bedroom with similar results. There were always orbs present while we helped the kids settle down and they disappeared when the kids fell asleep. In addition, they appeared in the master bedroom at the time I climbed into bed and they remained for several minutes until I started to drift off. I found it interesting that the orbs now moved into the master bedroom with me after I left the kids' room. Previously, they had shown no interest in what Monika and I did at night whenever the kids were not around.

On the evening of November 22, I spent several hours doing research on Mary Bell Wilson and her family. I poured over the papers I had copied at the Fort Collins Museum and studied the family portrait taken a few years before her death. I felt exhausted when I finished and left the papers out on my desk.

We held an impromptu communication that night in the kids' room as we tucked them in. Monika rested next to Becky and I sat on the floor beside Amanda's bed. Suddenly Monika started to speak.

"It is November 22, 2007, and we are here to communicate with the spirit of Mary Bell Wilson. Mary Bell, will you talk with us?"

To hear Monika reach out like this startled me. During previous communications, I had to prompt Monika in order to get her to say anything.

"Do you miss your daughter, Leona? I'll bet you were a good mother to Leona. Thank you for watching over our kids as they sleep."

Monika talked for several minutes. When she stopped, Michelle started to ask Mary Bell questions. I found it amusing that Michelle mimicked what I typically said during communications.

"Mary Bell," her quiet voice called from the top bunk bed, "will you let us see you in human form again? We want to see you the way you looked when you died."

I was both surprised and excited she asked this question. The anniversary of Mary Bell's death was approaching and I hoped we could make another psychic connection, and she would again manifest as a full-body apparition.

Shortly after Michelle asked her last question, the room fell silent because everyone had fallen asleep. I grabbed the video camera and left. Several weeks had passed since I had taken photographs in the kitchen and family room, so after dropping off the video camera in the master bedroom, I collected my digital camera and headed to the stairs. When I reached the landing, I heard a noise coming from the office below. It sounded like someone shuffling through loose papers. Curious, I leaned close to the railing and aimed the camera at the office. I snapped off four photographs before walking downstairs, where I took several pictures in the kitchen and family room.

When I reviewed the photographs, I found that two of the pictures taken inside the office were blurred; however, a solid cloud appeared in one of the two photos that turned out. This cloud was in front of my office chair near the computer. As I zoomed in on the image, the cloud took on the shape of a woman. The apparition was not as clear as the one in the September 10 picture, but I could make out the right arm and shoulder, the head and hair, and what appeared to be eyeglasses on the face. The ghost seemed to be looking up at me. Interestingly, the papers I heard shuffle just before taking this photo were my research notes about the Webster family, and the page on the top showed the photograph of the Webster family. Had the ghost recognized the people in the picture?

On the night of November 24, I had another encounter with our resident spirit. Usually I am the last one to bed, but on this night, I felt tired, so I was the first person to lie down. Before I climbed into bed, I positioned the video camera on the headboard behind me, aimed at the door, and started the tape. I had been in bed for about four minutes when Amanda came into the room. I got up to attend to her and then returned to bed. Approximately four minutes later, I heard two knocks on my headboard. My eyes flew open as I stopped breathing. Then I felt someone climb onto the bed on Monika's side and start to move toward me. I lay still, my heart thundering inside my chest. The presence crept up behind me and then I experienced the sensation of pressure on the lower half of my legs as if someone was lying on me. After several seconds, the pressure started to lift. At this time, I glanced at the foot of the bed and saw nothing. When I reviewed the videotape, I saw numerous orbs moving about the room as soon as I got in bed. The anomalies continued to appear until Amanda came into the room. They vanished while I attended to her and materialized once more after I returned to bed. Eight minutes into the tape, a white ball of light shot toward the head of the bed and two seconds later, the knocking occurs. Apparently, the ghost was responding to my earlier request to communicate through knocking. What was she trying to say? Was our ghost Mary Bell Wilson or someone else and why had the ghost suddenly taken an interest in what I was doing?

Chapter Ten

When I first contacted Susan Kniebes back in September regarding pioneer graves, she suggested that she come up to our house with her husband Duane so they could dowse in our yard for unmarked graves. Given the Kniebeses' long and successful history of finding graves on behalf of the Colorado Council of Genealogical Societies, I accepted their offer. We had planned to meet in October, but my back injury and a bout of bronchitis forced a delay. I stayed in touch with Susan via email, sending her updates whenever something exciting happened. Finally, we were able to set November 27 for our meeting. Joining us would be local historian and former genealogical society president, Cecilia Damschroder, and noted local historian and author Arlene Briggs Ahlbrandt.

The days leading up to our meeting were stressful. We needed to get the house ready for guests, which meant an industrial-strength cleaning. While I kept busy cleaning, I continued to film every night. My goal was to get the ghost to manifest in human form so I could capture this on video again.

I learned that some paranormal investigators claimed quartz crystals helped spirits appear. Apparently, under the right conditions, the energy captured by the quartz is released and this allows spirits to manifest. On November 26, I opted to try this. I purchased six quartz crystals from the Northern Lights spirituality store. The clerk at the store helped me find the crystals and then gave me directions on cleansing them.

"You can place them outside in moonlight or allow natural running water, such as water from a stream, to wash over them. By doing this it will release any negative energy that the quartz contained."

As she bagged my purchase, she handed me a card with her name on it and said she did tarot readings and that they made great Christmas gifts. I thanked her and quickly hustled out of the store.

When I arrived home, Sarah also told me that I needed to cleanse the crystals to release negative energy. Sarah, who has studied Wicca, is familiar with the powers of various stones and crystals. I just wanted to make our ghost show up in human form and if this meant I had to cleanse the crystals, then so be it. I was about to place the crystals in moonlight when Sarah hollered out the door.

"I wouldn't leave those outside. If we have any raccoons in the neighborhood, they are attracted to shiny objects."

The thought of missing out on a great ghost video because of a raccoon did not set well with me, so I brought my crystals inside and out of harm's way. Sarah said I could cleanse the crystals by passing them through the smoke of a frankincense incense candle. This sounded better than taking on a raccoon or making a late-night trip to the Poudre River.

Sarah gathered her incense burner and we made our way to the front porch, so the smoke would not linger inside the house. The temperature was hovering around forty degrees with wind out of the north. Between shivers, I managed to pass the crystals through the smoke, making them ready to transfer energy to our ghost. The only problem was they did not work as advertised. I took the stones into the kids' room as we tucked them into bed. Amanda fell asleep as soon as her head hit the pillow and Becky fell asleep soon after. For once, it was Michelle struggling to go to sleep. After about thirteen minutes of filming, Michelle leaned into my shoulder. "Dad, can I sleep with you and mom? My sisters always get to do it and I never do."

How could I refuse a request like that?

After Michelle piled onto our bed next to Monika, I retreated to the bathroom where I watched the tape. For the first eight minutes, there was steady orb activity, but not much after that. I set up the camera in the master bedroom and aimed it toward the door. I had been doing this every night for a week and had recorded orbs each time. I placed the crystals on a chair near the door, along with the paper, which displayed the Webster family portrait. When I watched the tape the next day, there was no activity inside the master bedroom. Did the crystals have a negative influence on the ghost? Perhaps I should have risked leaving them outside with the raccoons in order to cleanse them in moonlight.

On the morning of November 27, the house was abuzz with activity. Despite our best efforts at cleaning, we still had work to do. After putting most of the house in order, I had just enough time to take a quick shower before our guests arrived. Susan and Duane Kniebes were the first to show up. It was nice to be able to put a face to the name. I ushered them into the kitchen where I told them the story of how I first came to suspect that we had a ghost in our house. Cecilia Damschroder was the next to arrive, followed by local historian Arlene Ahlbrandt and her husband. I repeated my story. Cecilia listened without comment. I could tell she was the kind of person who absorbed information like a sponge and only made comments when she believed her input added to the conversation. From my previous phone conversations with Arlene, I knew she believed ghosts were real, and I could tell from her expression that she was happy to be there and review the evidence I had collected.

I set up five chairs in the office prior to our guests' arrival so they could watch my videos. After everyone settled in, I proceeded to play the video from our October 24 communication session. I chose this video for several reasons. First, I had started to leave a light on in the front office by this time, which improved the picture quality, and second, there was a high level of orb activity. On most videos, several minutes can pass between orb appearances and some people grow impatient waiting to see more action.

When the orbs started to show up on the video, Susan Kniebes appeared to be the most fascinated. She pointed to the orbs and discussed their appearance and movement. Cecilia did not understand what orbs were. I explained the three most popular theories regarding orbs, that they were either energy produced by living persons that ghosts used to manifest, energy produced by the ghost, or each orb represented an individual spirit. After watching approximately seven minutes of the video, Susan wondered if they could see something else. It is important to remember that none of these people specializes in paranormal studies. Their expertise was in historical research and documentation.

I next played part of the first video we made in the kids' room, which had a significant amount of orb activity. I chose this tape because I wanted them to see a video where the orbs interacted with us. After we watched a few minutes, I moved on to the September 10 videotape that showed the ghost floating in the kitchen. I was worried they may not be able to see the specter because it moves through the video quickly but they had no trouble seeing it. Susan Kniebes said, "Now that is what I think a ghost looks like."

The final tape I showed was the one shot in the master bedroom where the ghost knocked on the headboard of the bed. When I first played the tape, I somehow missed the part with the knocking and felt embarrassed as I tried to assure our guests that there was indeed knocking on the tape. Fortunately, I was able to locate the correct section and they each heard the knocking.

After we watched the videotapes, we discussed the history of the land. Cecilia Damschroder had done research on the area and suggested that our ghost could be connected to a Joseph Murray who had owned land close by. However, according to her notes, he did not stay in farming long, and by 1874 was the county assessor. Additionally, according to testimony from Leslie Williamson, no one from the Murray family was buried on the land the Murray family owned. Furthermore, the 1900 Great Western Sugar Map did not list Joseph Murray as a landowner in the Harmony District. We also discussed an interview Cecilia had conducted in 1995 with Charles Webster in which he told her that a wagon train had come through and several people on it suffered from the flu. Four of the people on the train had died and were buried. Her notes indicated these burials took place in the northeast corner of the Williamson property. This made sense because the Kniebeses had previously discovered graves in this area that did not belong to any members of the Williamson family. Leslie Williamson also stated that "a girl came through on a wagon and was hired as a maid by the Williamson family. She died soon after and was buried by the main gate." Apparently, this grave was unmarked. The data I had gathered to this point placed our subdivision on the Websters' land. Therefore, while the information regarding the girl's death and burial was interesting, I could not make a connection between what was happening at our house and the girl's death, unless Leslie Williamson had gotten the facts wrong and the girl was buried on the Websters' land.

After we discussed the history of the land, Arlene and her husband left. Susan then suggested we head outside where Duane could teach us how to use the dowsing rods while they conducted a search of our yard. In the backyard, Duane did a quick search around the middle of the yard before stopping. He then explained how the rods react to remains. "The rods can even react to cremated remains if the ashes have not been scattered. They also react to the remains of animals such as dogs. In addition to reacting to the energy that remains inside the bones of the dead, the rods also react to a living person's energy."

Duane proceeded to demonstrate this by having Cecilia sit and then pass the rods over her head. When he did this, the rods crossed.

"Whenever the rods are moved over a grave, they react in the same manner and cross."

He stepped back from Cecilia and the rods uncrossed. Duane then handed me a pair of rods. "Hold them loosely in your hands, approximately a half inch down from the point where the metal is bent, keeping your thumbs off the rods."

I knew from an email I had received from Robert Larson, president of the Larimer County Genealogical Society, that Duane had taught several members of their organization how to use the rods with success. Now armed with my new body-finding tool, I set off across the yard. My first stop was a location where I knew I would find bodies, the graves of two pet tortoises, Buster and Lucy, who had died over the summer and were now buried beneath a tree on the northeast corner of the yard. I stepped up to the graves with the rods extended. The rods bobbed slightly before gliding toward each other until crossing. I was stunned to discover that the rods actually worked. I turned toward the group.

"I just found a grave."

Susan's eyes widened. "You did?"

"Yes, this is where we buried our pet tortoises."

Her lips flattened into a grimace.

After my brief moment of fun, I started toward the southeast corner of our lot. As I approached the tree growing there, my hands begin to tingle as if an electrical current ran along the skin from my thumbs into my arms. This sensation grew stronger as I edged the rods closer to the tree. The rods started to sway and bob, and turn inward. As they did this, I felt energy moving through them. When they finally stopped, the rods had crossed to form an X. I turned toward the group. "I think I may have found something."

Duane ambled over to the spot and held out his rods. "Let's see what you've got here." His rods crossed instantly.

Monika, who also had a pair of rods, moved alongside him. Her rods crossed as well. Duane stood there for several seconds and then announced, "We may have something here."

I stepped back and watched as Duane stood over the spot concentrating. I knew from Robert Larson's email that Duane was asking questions of the buried individual via the rods. Duane stood there for approximately ten minutes before joining us.

"That is a gravesite. It belonged to a woman who died over a hundred years ago."

I was stunned and delighted by this latest discovery. "How can you tell the age of the grave?"

"When I communicated over the grave it took awhile to get a response. When a person has been dead for one hundred years or more, the response is slower, unlike recent deaths, where the response is quicker." Duane glanced back at the gravesite. "I'm having trouble getting a fix on which location the grave faces, but I don't want to walk out into the snow-covered bushes to get a better reading. If you go to a cemetery and hold the rods over the foot of a grave they will cross. If you then walk toward the headstone, they will uncross where the grave ends. By doing this you will know the size of the grave and thus have an idea of the size of the person buried. I'm having a hard time determining the size of this grave. The person may have been small."

"That would make sense," I told him. "When Monika saw the ghost upstairs, she said it was small, and the specter that appeared in the photograph taken inside the office also looked small. Plus, when we visited Mary Bell Wilson's grave, we discovered the area between the headstone and footstone was only about five feet."

I was curious about how Duane asks questions of buried individuals, so I pressed him for an explanation.

"The rods react over the grave by opening or closing in response to yes or no questions; for example, if you are holding crossed rods over the grave and said, 'If you are a woman, uncross the rods,' the rods should uncross if the body is that of a woman."

Susan and Duane left us with a pair of dowsing rods and suggested that we try asking questions over the gravesite. "Start out by asking, 'If the first letter of your name starts with the letter A, uncross the rods.' By doing this, you may be able to learn the ghost's identity. When you communicate with someone who has died, you can ask the question using only your mind. If you are using the rods with a living person, just ask the question aloud."

This advice made sense considering my own experience communicating telepathically with the ghost in our house.

"Duane has gotten so good at using the rods," Susan explained, "that we can go to a cemetery and he can walk up behind a headstone without seeing the inscription, and using the rods to ask questions he can learn the exact date of birth or death on the gravestone, as well as the person's name. Of course, this takes quite a while since he's limited to yes and no questions."

After the Kniebeses left our home, I returned to the backyard, dowsing rods in hand. As I moved the rods over the gravesite, I once again felt energy pulsating from my thumbs into the bottom half of my hands and radiating into my forearms. After the rods crossed, I telepathically inquired, "If you are a woman, uncross the rods." A few seconds passed and then the rods gradually moved apart.

This latest development stunned me. I had not expected the Kniebeses to find a grave in our backyard and I do not believe they had expected to either. After leaving, the Kniebeses set off to locate the two gravesites they had previously discovered on the Williamson property in 2001 using GPS. Since their last visit to the site, a housing development had gone up and they wondered if the graves were still there. Susan sent me an email saying they had discovered the graves located in the timbered area; however, the one located in a field was now in someone's front yard.

Later that evening, I tried an experiment with Monika. I held the dowsing rods over her head and they crossed. I then said, "If you love Ken, uncross the rods." The rods remained still for several nervous seconds before uncrossing. We repeated this experiment with Monika holding the rods over my head and asking, "If you love Monika, uncross the rods." Again, the rods uncrossed. Around 7:00 p.m., Monika and I tested the rods at the gravesite. A stiff wind dropped the temperature to near freezing. We both stood over the gravesite holding the dowsing rods. The rods crossed for both of us. I made several queries to the spirit. My first question was, "If you will be visiting our family inside the house tonight, uncross the rods." The rods pulsated slightly before uncrossing. I then said, "If you will let us see you in human form tonight, cross the rods." The rods jumped in my hands but did not cross. Later I inquired, "If you will ever let us see you again in human form, cross the rods." This time the rods crossed slowly.

That night I set up the video camera in the master bedroom on the headboard. We were going to bed later than I wanted and Michelle, Amanda, and Rebecca piled into bed with Monika and me. The girls were restless and fighting, so after about ten minutes we took them to their room. I brought the video camera and filmed in their room for eighteen minutes. During this time, I recorded a normal level of activity. Michelle and Rebecca went to sleep but Amanda ended up following me back to the master bedroom. I set up the camera on the headboard. During the first two minutes of tape several small white orbs twirled around in several directions, along with a couple of the more common ones that moved toward the headboard. During the remaining tape, I observed a couple of anomalies.

The next morning, I received a phone call from Charles Burchett. Charles lived just around the corner from our subdivision in a farmhouse on five acres of land. I had received his phone number from Susan Kniebes. Back in 2001, Charles helped the Kniebeses locate the

Williamson property, so I was hoping he might know the history of our subdivision's land. Charles was friendly and eager to share what information he knew. He told me the subdivision's land had indeed belonged to the Websters and they operated a sheep farm on it. He said the land was never developed and there were no buildings on it when Centex Homes purchased it. What he said next shocked me. According to Charles, he believed the house he lived in had belonged to the Webster family. Since I knew that Stewart Webster had built two homes on his property, this meant the house where Mary Bell Wilson had died still stood and was located approximately seventy yards from our house. This new evidence further supported the possibility that Mary Bell was our ghost. And because Mary Bell had lived with her husband approximately a half-mile west of her parents' house, it made sense she would have been buried in what is now our backyard, a location between the two houses. This still did not explain why we had so many orbs inside our house. If each orb contained a single spirit, we definitely had more than one ghost inside the house, and the fact that the photographs of the ghost taken on September 10 and November 22 appeared to be of different entities seemed to support this.

Chapter

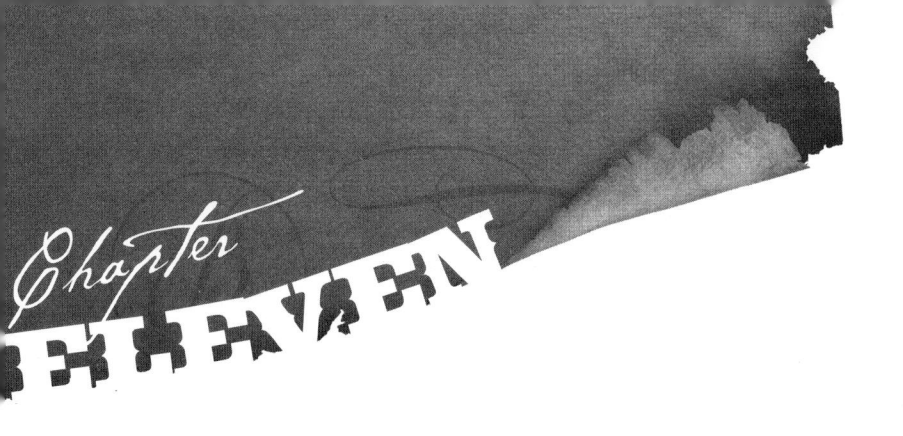

On the day after the Kniebeses visited, I used the dowsing rods over the gravesite in the backyard. My goal was to try to learn the identity of the person buried there. It was a typical late-November day with a lot of sunshine and a chill in the air. I waited until almost noon to go outside. Sarah was home from school, so she watched Amanda and Rebecca for me. I approached the gravesite holding the rods as instructed by Duane. As I moved the rods forward, they immediately swung together and crossed. A strong surge of energy raced through my hands as if from a small electric generator. My hands started to hurt so much I almost stopped.

I queried telepathically, "If your first name starts with the letter A, uncross the rods." I waited for over a minute without a response. I worked my way through the alphabet asking the same question. The rods did not move. When I said, "If your first name starts with the letter M, uncross the rods," the rods bobbed before swinging open. I immediately thought of Mary Bell Wilson. I next inquired, "If your last name starts with the letter W, cross the rods." Once again the rods responded, this time swinging together to cross. I then tried a more direct question. "If your husband was named Charles Wilson, uncross the rods." The rods immediately uncrossed. I next asked, "If you had a daughter named Leona, cross the rods," and the rods crossed.

I rushed into the house to find Sarah. "Sarah, Sarah, guess what?"

She sighed. "What?"

"When I used the rods over the grave and inquired if the spirit's name started with M, the rods moved. And then when I asked if their last name started with W, and they moved again. I immediately thought of Mary Bell. Then I inquired if the spirit had been married to Charles Wilson and the rods responded. Finally, I asked if the spirit had a daughter named Leona and the rods moved again."

Sarah did not look impressed. "Dad, Mary Bell probably just followed you outside."

If this was true, and our ghost was indeed Mary Bell Wilson, perhaps she could respond to questions inside the house. I walked into the entryway and stood with the rods aimed toward the stairs. The rods twitched in my hands but did not move. I then said telepathically, if the spirit of Mary Bell Wilson was present to cross the rods. Not only did the rods cross, they moved quickly and swung all the way around until hitting me. I rushed to the telephone and called Monika at work to tell her what happened. She was just as surprised as I was. When I got off the phone, I took the rods and returned to the bottom of the stairs.

The idea that I could communicate with someone dead for over one hundred twenty years was hard to fathom. You hear about these things happening with mediums, but I never imagined it could happen to me. Because the spirit identified itself as Mary Bell Wilson, I decided to verify its identity using questions only Mary Bell would be able to answer. My first question was, "If your father's name is Stewart, cross the rods." Once again, the rods quickly crossed and swung all the way around to hit my biceps. I wondered if the ghost would have enough strength to make the rods swing all the way back to uncross. I then said, "If your brother was named Samuel, uncross the rods." The rods twitched for a moment before slowly swinging around to uncross.

Over the next twenty minutes, I provided the following questions: Was your brother Samuel born in Missouri? Was your mother's name Margaret? Was Ruben your brother? Did you have a sister named Minnie? Each time the ghost answered correctly. I found it strange how the rods reacted based on the question asked. Sometimes they swung around quickly until coming back to hit my arms, and other times they moved slower. If the response was negative, the rods did not move at all. I had to stop communicating with the rods because of the discomfort in my hands. The ache did not subside for over an hour.

Based on the responses I received, I had every reason to believe the ghost was indeed Mary Bell Wilson. When my hands stopped hurting, I picked up the rods and returned to the bottom of the stairs. I elected to make queries that were not solely about her family. The inquiry was, "If you sometimes go somewhere to rest, cross the rods." The rods crossed without hesitation. I next asked if her family was with her and again the response was yes. I asked if Charles Wilson and Leona were with her, and the answer was positive. I then inquired, do you spend most of your time in the kids' bedroom? Answer: no. Do you spend most of your time in the master bedroom? Answer: yes. Are you buried at the Harmony Cemetery? Answer: yes. Do you visit your body sometimes? Answer: yes. Did you hold my hand last night after I requested you to? Answer: yes. (When we tucked the kids in their beds the night before, I was sitting on the floor next to Amanda's bed, and I asked Mary Bell telepathically if she could hold my hand. I put out my right hand and held it this way for several minutes. My goal was to find out if I would feel any kind of sensation. The only thing I felt was some tingling in my fingers). I then inquired, did you come and visit us last night? Answer: yes. Do you feel good this morning? Answer: yes. Can you see us? Answer: yes. Is the spirit of Ruben Webster inside this house? Answer: no. (I made this inquiry because Rebecca had told us that she saw Ruben's ghost in her bedroom). Is there more than one spirit living in this house? Answer: yes.

Rebecca came into the entryway and started to act up, making silly noises, and not allowing me to work. I scooped her up and gave her a pretend spanking. After putting her down, I picked up the dowsing rods and said the following: did you see me spank my daughter Rebecca? Answer: yes. Although Mary Bell had previously indicated that she could see us, I did not realize this meant she saw events in real-time. To test this, I next gave Mary Bell questions to learn exactly what she was seeing. The first questions concerned the clothes I was wearing (teal-green T-shirt, blue jeans, white tennis shoes). I started by giving her a trick question. If I am wearing a black shirt, uncross the rods. Answer: no. I then said if I am wearing a green shirt, uncross the rods. The rods immediately swung open. I next said if I am wearing white shoes, cross the rods. The rods crossed without hesitation.

Monika arrived home a short time later. I met her at the door and took her by the arm. "She can see me."

"What?"

"Mary Bell sees us as we walk around the house."

Monika's eyes narrowed. "What do you mean, she sees us?"

I proceeded to explain how Mary Bell identified the color of the clothes I wore.

"Wow, that's scary," Monika said. "Hey, why don't we take both pairs of dowsing rods and move upstairs to ask her some more questions?"

"All right."

We collected the second set of rods and went upstairs to the landing. I then held out my dowsing rods and said, "If Monika is wearing a black jacket, cross the rods." The rods crossed. I next tried to trick Mary Bell by inquiring if Monika wore white shoes. (She had on black shoes). Mary Bell correctly answered no. I then asked if Monika wore black shoes and the answer came back as yes.

We moved into the master bedroom. As we prepared to use the rods again, Rebecca came running into the room crying. I held out the rods and said, "If you can see my daughter crying, cross the rods." The rods crossed. "If my daughter Amanda is crying, uncross the rods." The rods remained motionless. "If my daughter Rebecca is crying, uncross the rods." The rods swung open.

These responses indicated that not only was the spirit of Mary Bell Wilson living with us, she watched as we went about our daily lives, and could identify us by name. Additionally, she had retained both her memory and intelligence.

A stricken expression crossed Monika's face. "Do you think she watches as we take our showers?"

"Probably so."

"I'm not crazy about that."

"What bothers me," I said, "is the idea that she has nothing better to do in the afterlife than watch us. How boring is that?"

Later that night, I used the rods again. I returned to my position at the bottom of the stairs and raised the rods. "If the spirit of Mary Bell Wilson is present, cross the rods."

The rods crossed without hesitation.

I asked Mary Bell several personal questions, which I believed she could not answer. "If my mother's name is Susan, uncross the rods." Answer: no. "If my mother's name is Jan, uncross the rods." Answer: yes. My mother's name is Jan. I decided to try a harder question. My mother's birth name was Ramona. She hated the name so much she had it legally changed when she was young. She did not even tell her children about her first name. I only knew what it was because my older brother stumbled across a copy of her birth certificate while we were visiting our grandfather. "If my mother's name used to be Ramona, cross the rods." The rods reacted immediately to cross. "If my grandmother's name is Katharine, uncross the rods." I do not have a grandmother named Katharine and Mary Bell answered correctly. "If my grandmother's name was Ollie, uncross the rods." The rods uncrossed to correctly answer. "If my grandmother Ollie is buried in Fort Collins, cross the rods." The rods remained motionless, which is correct. She is buried in El Paso, Texas. "If my grandmother Ollie is buried in El Paso, cross the rods." The rods crossed.

How was it possible for a ghost to know this information? This certainly was not something we discussed around the house. My next question was, "If I have a daughter named Julie, uncross the rods." Mary Bell correctly answered no. When I inquired if I had daughters named Sarah and Michelle, Mary Bell correctly said yes. I changed the line of questioning. "If you knocked on my headboard the other night, uncross the rods." Answer: yes. "If you climbed onto my bed, cross the rods." Answer: yes. By this time, my hands started to ache once more, so I ended the communication.

Two days later, on the afternoon of November 30, we returned to the Harmony Cemetery to visit Mary Bell Wilson's grave, this time with the dowsing rods. When we arrived, the sky was stone gray, and a crisp wind scattered leaves as we walked across the cemetery grounds. I first approached the grave from the back of the headstone. Holding out the rods, I expected to experience a strong physical reaction, such as I did when approaching the gravesite in our backyard. However, I felt no strong current pulsating through my hands and the rods did not cross. Monika took a position at the foot of the grave. When she held out the rods, they crossed. I joined her and my rods crossed, but the energy coming from the grave was not strong. We attempted to perform a spiritual dowsing, which unlike dowsing to locate a gravesite, involves the use of the rods to contact a spirit for communication. The rods responded weakly to questions such as, "Is your name Mary Bell Wilson?" The overall impression both Monika and I came away with was that Mary Bell's spirit was not present.

Because we now knew the identity of the ghost in our house, our relationship with her changed and we no longer feared her presence. In a strange way, she became like a part of our family. We left the cemetery and headed home, confident Mary Bell was there waiting for us.

Chapter Twelve

On December 1, Sarah became the second person in our household to see Mary Bell's ghost. What makes this incident unusual is that it occurred during the day. It was a Saturday morning and Sarah had to go to work at Ace Hardware. Around 8:30, she started upstairs to finish getting ready. Monika was in bed with Amanda and Rebecca in the master bedroom, and Michelle was asleep in the kids' room. As Sarah walked up the stairs, she saw a small white figure glide from the kids' room toward the master bedroom. At first, she thought it might have been Michelle, but when Sarah checked in the kids' room, she found Michelle sleeping on the top bunk. She then looked in the master bedroom and saw that everyone was asleep.

Sarah, who had avoided involving herself in my investigation, did not report the sighting until returning home from work.

As Christmas approached, the focus of my investigation changed. I made a decision to try filming downstairs again instead of in the master bedroom. Filming in the master bedroom, I captured orbs every night, and filmed the incident where Mary Bell knocked on the headboard, but I wanted more. Because I filmed in low light on September 10 when Mary Bell floated in the kitchen, the resulting image was not as clear as I hoped. My new goal was to capture Mary Bell on video again, only this time with backlighting. To do this, I knew we needed to hold communications again.

On December 10, around 11:30 p.m., I set up the video camera in the kitchen, aimed at the sliding glass door. I chose not to hold a communication because Monika and the girls had already gone upstairs. Instead, I made a psychic connection with Mary Bell using the dowsing rods prior to filming. Standing in the entryway with the rods pointed at the stairs, I felt energy pulsating along the bottom of my hands. I said if the spirit of Mary Bell Wilson was present for her to cross the rods. The ends of the rods bobbed before swinging together to cross. I next said, "If you're going to visit us tonight, uncross the rods." The rods uncrossed. "If you're going to let us see you in human form, cross the rods." The rods bobbed once more and began to move together, only to pull back before crossing. It appeared Mary Bell was hesitating, but after about a minute, the rods crossed weakly at the tips. My final question was, "If your family is with you now, uncross the rods." The rods opened without hesitation. After I finished, I started the video camera and went upstairs.

I had a restless night. As I started to fall asleep, I felt a thump on the side of my left foot, as if someone had swatted it with their hand. I sat up and looked at Monika to see if she had kicked me, but she was asleep, her feet about forty inches from mine. I lay back down and closed my eyes. Suddenly I experienced the sensation of someone climbing onto the foot of the bed. I glanced at the end of the bed but saw nothing.

Throughout the night, it felt as though I never fell asleep. I remembered glancing around the room at various times. I sensed the presence of two spirits in the room, one being Mary Bell, and the other one unknown, but possibly a man. They tried to communicate with me. I heard one of them speaking, but I do not know what they said. They seemed to be discussing the dowsing rods, and at one point, I saw the unidentified spirit holding a pair of dowsing rods, staring at them intently. Sarah came into my room around 7 a.m. to tell me about a problem with her toilet. My eyes flew open and I said, "The spirits have been talking to me all night." As I climbed out of bed, I felt fatigued and had a headache.

When I reviewed the videotape shot downstairs, I heard a strange noise that started at the beginning of the tape and lasted for the first six minutes. It was a crinkling noise, like someone crushing cellophane paper. An orb appeared three minutes into the tape, with several more materializing later, including one bright sphere. At numerous points, small white balls of light showed up, and at forty-five minutes, several large orbs appeared.

The next night after I prepared the video camera downstairs, I used the dowsing rods. According to numerous ghost hunters, dowsing rods are one of the oldest ghost hunting devices. Investigators claimed that in the presence of a spirit, the spirit's ambient energy will cause a reaction in the rods and they would cross in the same manner as when used for spirit communication. Up to this point, the rods had only crossed while being moved over the gravesite in the backyard or inside the house after I asked Mary Bell a question. On this night, as I held out the rods near the sliding glass door, they started to bob and swung together to cross before I had an opportunity to ask anything. I then said, "If the spirit of Mary Bell Wilson is present, uncross the rods." The rods uncrossed. I provided a few more questions including, "If you will allow us to see you again in human form." The response was positive.

When I reviewed the video, I observed electrical interference at the start. Sarah later told me her clock radio had awakened her for three consecutive nights by making a loud grinding noise. This activity led me to believe Mary Bell was preparing to make another appearance in human form. Unfortunately, I had no idea where to film. Should I concentrate my efforts downstairs in the kitchen where Mary Bell had appeared back in September, or upstairs? The December 10 video filmed in the kitchen had orbs present at various times, but in subsequent videos filmed over the next several nights, there were none. As on previous tapes, it appeared Mary Bell had no interest in hanging around the kitchen while we slept upstairs.

There had been an extreme increase in the level of ghost activity after I started to use the dowsing rods to communicate with Mary Bell. Once she realized we were capable of talking with her, she wanted to make her presence known to us. I was having more and more dreams in which her spirit tried to communicate. Additionally, she seemed to be responding to my request to communicate by knocking or making some kind of noise.

On the afternoon of December 13, around one o'clock, I was in the kitchen, while Amanda and Rebecca played in the family room. Suddenly, a rocking horse music box on top of a bookcase started to play. The music box played for five seconds before stopping. I immediately examined the music box and found it rocking. We had played this heavy ceramic music box less than ten times and it was in mint condition. It has a key on the bottom and does not play music unless someone winds the key, and will only rock if manipulated by hand.

On December 16 at about 11:00 p.m., I was sitting at my desk in the office when Sarah came downstairs.

"Dad, someone keeps coming into my room while I'm sleeping and turning on my heater. It heats my room up to like ninety-five and I wake up sweating."

Sarah's room is the coldest inside the house so she sometimes uses a portable heater.

"What do you think is causing that?" I said.

"I think Amanda is sneaking into my room."

"Sarah, I seriously doubt your four-year-old sister is sneaking into your room at night to turn on your heater. I'll bet Mary Bell is doing it."

Sarah threw up her hands. "You always blame things on the ghost, but I don't believe it."

After she went back to her room, I walked into the kitchen and started the video camera. I moved close to the sliding glass door and held out the dowsing rods. They soon crossed on their own without prompting. The first question I always ask is if the spirit of Mary Bell Wilson is present. Once I established that she was present, I inquired if she would be visiting us tonight after we went to bed and her response was yes. I then asked if she would allow us to see her in human form, and again she said yes. I explained to Mary Bell that it was important for us to see her as she appeared while alive. When I finished, I headed upstairs. At the landing, I noticed that the door to the kids' room was closed. I knew the room was unoccupied because the girls had piled in bed with Monika. For some reason, I felt compelled to open the door, even though I was not filming upstairs. It took me a while to fall asleep and at 11:40, I heard Sarah leave her room and go into the bathroom. A minute later, I heard her leave the bathroom followed by her bedroom door closing with a thud. Soon after, I felt the sensation of someone climbing onto my bed and advancing until straddling my legs. A feeling of pressure started to move in the direction of my chest, followed by a rush of cold that swept over me. The pressure gradually dissipated around my waist.

The next morning when I started downstairs, I found Sarah sitting at the computer in the office. She looked up at me, a serious expression on her face. "I saw the ghost last night."

I chuckled and said, "I told you she was the one who turned on your heater. What happened?"

"Well, I was in my room reading and got up to use the bathroom. Normally, I always turn on the hall light, but for someone reason, I didn't. I was in the bathroom for about a minute and then came out. When I reached my sisters' room, I glanced toward their door because I noticed it was open. Mary Bell suddenly materialized in the open doorway, close to my face."

"What did she look like?"

"I'd say she was between 5'2" and 5'4", wearing a white floor-length dress that had long sleeves. She appeared for about a second before vanishing."

This was the second time in less than a month Sarah had seen Mary Bell and the closest anyone had been to her when she materialized. I wondered if Mary Bell chose to appear before Sarah because I had asked her to let us see her in human form. Or did she do this because Sarah expressed skepticism regarding Mary Bell's ability to influence her surroundings?

Around 9:00 p.m., December 17, Sarah was using the computer downstairs when she heard the familiar grinding sound that accompanied Mary Bell absorbing energy. This happened again at 10:45 p.m. on the clock radio in her bedroom while I was talking to her. I opted to film upstairs with the camera aimed toward the kids' room with their door left open. I did not use the dowsing rods to contact Mary Bell prior to filming. The only activity recorded was a single orb at the start of the video near Sarah's closed door.

The next night we went to my parents' house to help wrap Christmas presents. After spending several hours at their house, I shuttled Monika, Michelle, Amanda, and Rebecca home in our rental car. A few days earlier,

Monika had lost control of our van on an icy road and slammed into the curb. While the van was being repaired, we had to use a rented Toyota Camry, and it was not large enough to accommodate the six of us. I dropped them off at our house around 11:30 p.m. and drove back to my parents' house to pick up Sarah. When Sarah and I arrived back home, Monika met us at the door, her face flushed. "I have to tell you what happened while you were gone."

"What?"

"I was in the family room with the kids and Amanda and Rebecca were being really naughty. They ran around acting crazy. I became frustrated and shouted, 'Mary Bell, your angry spirit probably got into the kids.' A few seconds later, I heard a loud banging sound that came from the stairs. When I checked, I found two of the pictures on the ground at the bottom of the stairs. I went ahead and hung the pictures back up."

I walked to the stairs to examine the pictures, which are actually wooden frames that displayed family photographs, covered by glass. Three hung together on the wall going up the stairs. The two largest frames had crashed down. The biggest measured forty-eight by twelve inches, and the other was twelve by twelve. The larger frame had some damage to the wood, but the glass remained undamaged on both pictures.

When Monika told me this story, I had a hard time believing it. There was no logical explanation for the frames to come crashing down. They had been hanging on the wall for six months on heavy-duty hooks. When I examined the back of the frames, I found them undamaged, as were the hooks on the wall.

That night I filmed upstairs. The kids slept in their room for a change and I aimed the camera toward their open door. After starting the camera, I turned off the lights and went in the room with the girls to settle them down. I took my usual position on the floor beside Amanda's bed. As I was sitting, I became aware of a cold spot over my right shoulder. I had never experienced this while in their room. I reached out with my right hand and noted that the spot extended into the middle of the room. Michelle and Rebecca fell asleep right away but Amanda ended up going with me to our room. I left the door to the kids' room open when I left. The next morning upon reviewing the tape, I saw several orbs in the hallway, but unfortunately, right after I took Amanda into the master bedroom, Sarah came out into the hallway and closed the door into the kids' room, which was not surprising considering her experience the previous night.

The next evening, we went Christmas shopping. Sarah stayed home alone. She remained in her bedroom with the door closed and all the downstairs lights turned on. At approximately 8:40 p.m., my cell phone rang.

"Dad," Sarah said a hint of fear in her voice.

"What is it?"

"I just heard a loud crash coming from downstairs."

"What was it?"

"I don't know," she said, "I'm not leaving my room to investigate."

"All right, we're on our way home and should be there in about five minutes."

When we arrived home, I discovered the twelve by twelve picture frame at the base of the stairs. Once more, I examined the picture frame and wall hook prior to hanging it back up and found them both in perfect condition.

I had not communicated with Mary Bell for a few days and suspected the picture throwing was her way of letting us know we should not ignore her. I considered contacting her with the dowsing rods but decided against it because I wanted to see how she would respond if I did not communicate with her. That night, I set up one of the cameras aimed toward the stairs with the hope of capturing Mary Bell throwing a picture off the wall. Unfortunately, nothing happened on the video. I did however have the feeling that Mary Bell and other spirits visited with me while I slept. Once again, I awoke with a headache and feeling exhausted.

On December 20, I was downstairs late with Amanda and Rebecca because they could not sleep. Finally, after getting them to bed, I returned to the kitchen. Around 3:40 a.m., I was standing in the kitchen with all the lights turned on, when an orb materialized in front of me. It was slightly larger than a ping-pong ball, tan with brown swirls, and ringed in a royal blue color. The orb appeared glossy and wet. It hovered in front of me for about two seconds before vanishing. I quickly turned to my right, and the orb appeared in front of me again. It remained for two more seconds before disappearing. This was the first and only time I saw an orb with my eyes.

I grabbed the dowsing rods to contact Mary Bell. The rods immediately swung together and crossed. A strong current of energy surged through my hands. After establishing that Mary Bell was with me, I said, "Mary Bell, if you knocked the pictures off the wall, cross the rods." Her response was positive. I then inquired, "Did you knock the pictures off the wall because you were angry with me for not communicating with you for a few days?" Again, her answer was yes. I questioned if she remained upset with me and her answer was no. My next question was, "Have you been visiting me in my dreams?" She answered yes. I questioned Mary Bell if she sometimes visited Monika in her dreams and the response was no. I then said, "Are you going to be visiting me tonight in my room?" Answer: yes. "Will you be climbing up onto the bed?" Answer: yes.

When I finished communicating with Mary Bell, I went to bed. Not long after I lay down, I felt someone climb onto the bed and straddle my legs. Once more, I looked toward the foot of the bed but saw nothing. After I fell asleep, I again sensed that spirits were in the room and trying to communicate with me. While this happened, I was aware of my surroundings. I saw the inside of the master bedroom and could make out the furniture. I saw the spirits, but they remained far enough away to make identification impossible. I have never experienced recurring dreams in the past, but this dream, if that is what it was, happened frequently, sometimes several nights in a row. On this night, I had the sensation of leaving my body and flying while surrounded by spirits.

With Christmas fast approaching, we became busy with last-minute shopping and preparations. As a result, my investigation slowed. I continued to film upstairs and occasionally did a short communication prior to going to bed. One night, after a particularly long and tiring day, I told Mary Bell that I was exhausted and hoped to have a good night's sleep. No spirits visited and I slept soundly.

On the night of December 23, I had an unusual dream involving a deceased family pet. The dream did not involve Mary Bell or anything that was happening inside our house, but it did make me wonder if spirits communicated with the living as we slept, as theorized by many mediums and paranormal researchers. Back in 2004, I had a dream in which I saw my late grandmother Ollie Harmon and our pet cockatiel Snowbird, who died in 2000. During the dream, Snowbird dove into a cup of water. When cockatiels get wet, they are extremely ugly. You can see through their feathers all the way to their bony wings and red skin. In my dream, when she emerged from the water, her wings were fluffed and dry and she looked beautiful. In my dream on December 23, I was inside a bright all-white room with a rectangular pool off to one side. I saw bubbles on the surface of the water and then suddenly our poodle Jeff popped out of the water. He stood with his front paws on the edge of the pool, wagging his tail. He looked young and vigorous, not like the last time I saw him shortly before his death in 1990. I had not dreamed about him since his death. What stood out to me about this dream was the image of water. Water played a part in both this dream and the dream in which I saw Snowbird. Did water represent the boundary between the animal spirit world and that of humans?

I took time off from the investigation on Christmas Eve and Christmas Day. On the night of December 26, I filmed inside the kids' room for the first time in about a month. The girls fell asleep right away and I only filmed for eight minutes. During that time, I filmed a single orb. When I left the kids' room, I went downstairs to work on the computer. I finally went to bed at 3:30 a.m. In the master bedroom, I set up the video camera on the nightstand. I started the camera before going into the bathroom. When I came out several minutes later, I undressed and climbed into bed. Upon reviewing the tape, I observed no activity while I was inside the bathroom, but as soon as I climbed into bed, orbs started to fly. I counted fifty in the first eight minutes of tape. At one point, five of them flew toward the bed at the same time. They were various sizes and brightness levels. Some moved toward the bed, others away from the bed, and some changed direction. They also moved at various speeds, some traveling at low speeds, others streaked across the room.

Over the next two nights, I recorded an unusually high level of anomalies in the master bedroom every time I went to bed. If each orb represented a single spirit, we had the entire Webster family living with us.

Chapter Thirteen

I first came across Mark Macy's name on Google while searching for a way to communicate with spirits. Prior to 1988, Macy had been an atheist who believed the idea of an afterlife was wishful thinking. Then he nearly died from colon cancer. After making a recovery, he investigated the possibility of life after death. Macy learned about ITC research (instrumental transcommunication) conducted by investigators such as the Harsch-Fischbach couple of Luxembourg and George Meek of North Carolina. After studying their work, Macy became convinced of the existence of life after death and soon immersed himself in this science, which uses common electrical devices such as telephones, radios, televisions, and computers to contact and communicate with spirits and angels. According to Macy, researchers have received information from Thomas Edison, Albert Einstein, and others who are alive, well, and communicating from the world of spirits. It is Macy's belief that when the physical body dies our mind lives on with a view of far greater depth and clarity.

Macy believes there are countless subtle worlds beyond the physical world we know, each teeming with life, and while the many worlds of spirits all inhabit the same space; each realm remains distinct by its vibration of consciousness that makes each realm of existence unique and discrete. He also says we should not assume that only psychics, spiritualists, and schizophrenics could make contact with the spirit realms. Macy feels that we all tune in to some of those realms in our dreams, something I had experienced for myself.

While conducting his research, Macy acquired a laminator. He uses this machine to take Polaroid photographs that reveal the spirits of people who have died. According to Macy, the laminator establishes a field of subtle energy that melts away the boundary between the physical world and rather dense spiritual worlds that are close by in vibration. It allows people in spirit to come unusually close to us and draw upon our bodily substances (what spiritualists call ectoplasm), so the spirit people can become denser than usual—dense enough to show up on the Polaroid film—but still remain just out of the range of normal human vision.

When I contacted Macy back in October, I was hoping he could give me advice on how to communicate with the ghost in our house. I found his work with the laminator interesting, and when I learned he had grown up in Windsor, Colorado, which is about four miles from our house, I sent him an email. When Macy replied, he agreed we probably had what he called a "stuck spirit." He suggested that I do not try to communicate with it, especially if I had kids. He went on to say:

Stuck spirits are usually stuck because they're confused and/or full of fear or resentment or some other low-vibration emotions. When you communicate with people with such emotions (on either side of the veil), you tend to lower your vibration to match theirs, and in doing so you tend to invite such spirits into your life and your family. The purpose of true ITC is to open communication channels to spirits and ethereal beings that are stable and settled in fine worlds of spirits. They're the ones who can give information to help our world and support us in our lives. In regards to communicating with the spirit you seem to have in your house, my suggestion would be just to pray. Commune with guides and guardians, and ask them along with ethereal beings, to help locate the stuck spirit and raise her to a finer vibration where she can be "rehabilitated." Ask the same finer spirit

> *beings to support and protect you and your family. That's the only communication I'd recommend in this case. I think ghost hunting is a good cause only when the intention is to help the spirits get settled and redeemed... or "unstuck."*

I received Macy's advice in October, but after carefully considering his warning, I elected to go ahead and attempt to communicate with Mary Bell. By this time, I was deep into my investigation and had already made contact with Mary Bell. In addition, my investigation did not seem to be having a negative impact on our kids, and if I had any reason to believe it was, I would not have gone forward. No one in my family considered Mary Bell a threat. I also wondered if she was in fact in a "stuck state," awaiting assistance to move to another realm. However, I knew that Macy had many years of investigative experience, so I kept his advice in the back of my mind before launching into my ITC experiment.

While I believed ITC represented a better opportunity for contacting a spirit than a Ouija board, I still did not have confidence in the use of ITC for our case. Why would a person not related to us, who had been dead over one hundred twenty-one years want to make contact through an electronic device? Still, I chose to try ITC to see if it would work with Mary Bell.

I had attempted ITC once before with disastrous results. Not only did the video camera fail to capture anything when aimed toward our big-screen TV in the family room, an odd dark streak appeared on the lower right corner of the screen. When the repair technician replaced the two inner panels, he was stunned to discover that the streak was a slimy film located between the panels.

"These panels are sealed so nothing should be able to penetrate them and get inside," he said. "I've only seen one other case like this. A wisp of smoke somehow managed to work its way inside the television, but no one here smokes, right?"

"That's right," I said.

"And even if you did smoke, that wouldn't explain this slimy film."

My goals for using ITC were twofold. I hoped to capture the image and voice of Mary Bell on the television and I wanted to find out if she was a "stuck spirit." If she were stuck, I would do whatever I could to help her move on to the proper realm. I planned to use ITC for a period of four weeks to try to contact Mary Bell. If I had no success by that time, I intended to try using ITC to contact my late grandmother. Many people who study ghosts believe spirits were not intended to remain closely attached to the living as J. Allan Danelek explains in his book *The Case for Ghosts*. "It also seems likely that most people will never become a ghost but will instead choose to move on immediately after they die, precisely as they were designed to do." If this were true, would my grandmother respond to my request to communicate?

Using ITC to contact spirits should not be difficult. As Danelek states, "the average person may be surprised to learn that communicating with the dead may be easier than one might think and, further, that it requires no special training, equipment, or inherent paranormal powers to do so. All it takes is an openness to such communication being a possibility, some patience, and perseverance, and the rest will take care of itself."

My biggest obstacle in conducting ITC experiments was that I needed to work around the schedules of everyone in the house. I had originally planned to start the experiments over Christmas break, but the kids enjoyed staying up late and I needed a quiet environment. I was finally able to start on January 3, 2008, after I personally escorted the girls into their bedroom to get them to fall asleep at a decent hour. I had not filmed in their bedroom for a week and the last time I did film, I only recorded a single orb.

After reading the girls a book, I turned out the light and sat on the floor next to Amanda's bed. As usual, Rebecca and Michelle fell slept quickly but Amanda stayed awake. I rewound the tape and watched with Amanda in their room. There was little orb activity. Near the end of the tape, we heard a loud crash. Sarah came out of her room. "Did you hear that noise?"

"I think it came from outside the house," I said.

"From my room it sounded like it came from the kitchen."

Sarah accompanied me as we searched downstairs. We were unable to find the source of the sound.

I had Sarah watch Amanda while I tried to communicate with Mary Bell on the television in the office. I placed the television on "input two" in order to create "white noise" on the screen and then started the camera. I began by providing a brief history of my previous attempts at communicating with Mary Bell. Approximately ten seconds into the film, the television turned off. After restarting the television, I asked questions such as, "Mary Bell Wilson, are you here with me tonight?" "Can you let me see you?" and "can you give us a glimpse of the spirit world," etc. I filmed for fifteen minutes. As I rewound the tape, the television turned off again.

As I watched the tape, I did not observe anything unusual. The closest she came to appearing was near the end of the tape when a vertical line materialized and shimmered back and forth across the screen for several seconds. In addition, no Electronic Voice Phenomena (EVP) were detected during the session. EVP are responses from the deceased that cannot be heard in real time as the questions are asked, but can be captured by a recorder and reviewed after the fact. The results did not surprise me because I had learned that it might take several weeks to achieve results using this method.

Prior to trying ITC on the next night, I used the dowsing rods to make a connection with Mary Bell. After making contact, I inquired if she had turned off the television the previous evening. The answer was yes. I then explained that I was trying a new method of communicating with her and that it might be possible for me to see her face and hear her voice. I told her she would need to concentrate in order to make this work. Amanda was still awake so I asked Mary Bell if it was all right for Amanda to be present, and she said yes. I then told her I was going to move into the office and implored her to accompany me.

Amanda fell asleep right away, so the room was quiet as I conducted the communication. I made a change in the experiment by setting the television on a channel not used for broadcasting and switched the input setting to "input one." This created a blue background instead of the white-and-black background associated with white noise. The blue background was easier to watch, and according to people who had success with ITC, it did not matter what background I used as long as the TV was on a channel that did not receive signals. Once again, I asked questions for fifteen minutes, only this time, I implored Mary Bell to concentrate in order to materialize.

Unfortunately, the results were the same with no unusual activity recorded.

Prior to my third attempt at ITC, I again used the dowsing rods to contact Mary Bell before moving into the office where I repeated the previous experiment with the same result. The television did shut off at one point, but this was the only event of significance. I opted not to contact Mary Bell with the dowsing rods prior to filming the next night.

While I conducted the ITC experiments, I continued to film upstairs. I placed one camera in the hallway between the bedrooms and the other camera on our headboard in the master bedroom. The camera in the hallway was not getting results, but the master bedroom camera recorded a moderate amount of orbs. I always started the camera before I went into the bathroom, but it did not record orbs until I returned to bed. At that point, the orbs started to fly and continued at a steady pace for several minutes. My goal continued to be capturing Mary Bell in full manifestation; however, I was starting to believe this was not going to happen in the master bedroom, so I began to make plans to resume filming in the kitchen.

From a psychological standpoint, attempting to communicate with a ghost is frustrating. You can try to make a connection night after night without results and just when you feel like giving up, something happens that makes you continue.

On the night of January 10, I was not able to do the ITC experiment because Monika went to bed early and left me to watch Amanda and Rebecca. I tried to put them to bed, but it soon became apparent they were not going to wind down, so I brought them into bed with Monika and me. After I got them to lie down, I started the video camera and climbed into bed. I took several photographs with the digital camera. I then stretched out under the sheets. As I lay with my eyes closed, this thought went through my mind—Mary Bell would never materialize in human form in the master bedroom because she had never tried to take energy from the video camera in this location. When I reviewed the video the next day, I saw multiple orbs in the first several minutes. Five minutes into the tape, I heard the familiar grinding noise that occurred whenever Mary Bell gathered energy. Had she read my thoughts and decided to prove me wrong?

I resumed the ITC experiment the following evening. Because it was a Friday night, I was able to film late. I taped for fifteen minutes, and while I did not record any images or audio evidence, I noticed more activity on the screen. By activity I mean minute changes, for example, colors darkening, variations in the vibrations, etc. These changes gave me hope that the ITC experiment would prove successful.

I continued the ITC experiments, but by the end of February, it became clear that Mary Bell was not going to respond to this method of communication. I do not know if this was because I had already established a connection with her using the dowsing rods or if she just did not feel comfortable communicating this way. Perhaps she just did not want me to see her on the television. I am the one who had spent the most time communicating with Mary Bell and I am the only one she had reached out to in dreams, and yet, I have never seen her in human form, even when she was only a few feet from me.

Back on December 30, I received an email from J. Allan Danelek, author of *A Case for Ghosts*, in which he stated, "All I can say is that once a person establishes a relationship with a discarnate personality (ghost) they often tend to become more brazen in their efforts at getting your attention. If you are actually in contact with the spirit of this young woman, don't be surprised if she actually becomes infatuated with you personally and perhaps even grows jealous if you don't continue to respond to her." Prior to receiving Danelek's email, I had never considered the possibility of establishing a relationship with Mary Bell. I wondered if Mary Bell chose to hide from me out of embarrassment because she considered me a friend, or perhaps because I was the only male in our household. Whatever the reason, she did not appear or attempt to communicate with me during the ITC experiment, therefore, I concluded that if I were ever going to get answers about the afterlife from Mary Bell, I would have to use the dowsing rods.

Chapter Fourteen

I had many questions I wanted to ask Mary Bell about death and the afterlife. My plan involved asking a series of prepared questions using the dowsing rods.

My purpose for using the dowsing rods was to gain knowledge from the living spirit of Mary Bell Wilson and to assist her in crossing over to the proper realm, if evidence confirmed she was stuck in the wrong place. Because a ghost answers by maneuvering the rods, I was limited to asking yes or no questions.

The first problem I faced prior to holding the dowsing sessions was to determine the best location. When I first contacted Mary Bell, I stood in the entryway with the rods pointed toward the stairs. However, I had successfully made contact in a number of places including the kitchen, family room, upstairs landing, and master bedroom. I finally chose the spot near the stairs because the last time I made contact with Mary Bell in this area, I received a strong response.

My next decision involved choosing what questions to ask. To identify the spirit as Mary Bell, I planned to ask questions regarding her family and life in Fort Collins back in 1886. I then would ask questions regarding her death, and finally, the afterlife and spirit world.

On the evening of April 11, I attempted to communicate with Mary Bell through the dowsing rods, but she was a no-show. I did feel movement in the rods when I asked if she was present, but they never came close to crossing. This initial failure confirmed two things:

1. Ghosts are unpredictable.

2. If my subconscious mind caused the dowsing rods to move as skeptics suggested, then the rods should have crossed when I asked Mary Bell to do this.

I had several communications with Mary Bell in the days prior to April 11, so I was surprised when she did not respond; however, I have never believed that she was always present inside our house. I opted to make another attempt later in the evening. Just after midnight, on April 12, I started in the same place at the bottom of the stairs. This time, I made a connection right away and the rods crossed before I could ask Mary Bell if she was present. I then questioned her for an hour before stopping.

I started by establishing that the spirit of Mary Bell Wilson was there. Once the rods reacted to indicate a positive answer, I moved forward with the inquires. Mary Bell confirmed that she died in 1886. She next affirmed she had been married to Charles Wilson. I had previously queried Mary Bell if she had been happily married to Charles, and the answer was no. I found nothing in my research of the family history that would explain her answer. Perhaps Mary Bell did not enjoy living on a farm. I knew from reading an old newspaper article that three strangers had attacked her husband and burned one of the buildings on their farm. Charles Wilson did not raise their daughter Leona after Mary Bell's death, and he remarried within a couple of years. However, he did pay for Mary Bell's cemetery plot and headstone.

Mary Bell next confirmed her father was Stewart Webster. The rods responded immediately, and swung all the way around until hitting my shoulders. The rods moved in the same manner to indicate yes when I asked if Margaret Webster was her mother. I knew from my research that Stewart Webster raised sheep, but I had never asked Mary Bell if she lived on a farm. Mary Bell acknowledged that she had. While interviewing Mary Bell, I sometimes used trick questions to see if she would answer incorrectly. The first time I did this was to inquire if her family raised cattle on their farm, knowing they did not. Mary Bell answered correctly.

Mary Bell lived in the section of Fort Collins known as the Harmony District, an area several miles from downtown that consisted of numerous family farms. According to Mary Bell's responses, the people who resided there were a close-knit community. Mary Bell's younger sister Minnie Webster married David Williamson, who owned the adjoining farm. I next shifted the focus to Mary Bell's illness from typhoid fever and her resulting death. Mary Bell remembered becoming sick. Her answer surprised me since victims of typhoid fever become delirious in the final stages. I next asked if she remembered dying, and her answer was no. The rods started to move together to indicate a positive response, but never crossed. I can only assume that the question was too vague because when I next asked if she went into a dark tunnel when she died, Mary Bell did not hesitate to give a positive response. She also indicated she had moved toward a bright light. Does this light represent a new birth, or a passage into heaven? Astronomer Carl Sagan hypothesized that people having near-death experiences were actually re-living perinatal experiences. Dr. Raymond Moody discovered similarities between the two experiences while researching near-death experiences—a rapid movement toward and/or sudden immersion in a powerful light.

I continued my inquiries about the dying process. I next asked Mary Bell if she saw moments from her life as she died, and Mary Bell answered yes. This question proved difficult to phrase, but Mary Bell answered without hesitation. Viewing scenes from their lives is another phenomenon reported during near-death experiences. My personal belief is the dying view memories of their past lives as they pass into the soul before it leaves the body. Mary Bell acknowledged that she remained in her parents' house when she came into the bright light. What does this mean? Do all of us remain in the same place when we die, only in a different physical state, or did Mary Bell fail to cross over to the proper spirit realm and was now stuck? Mary Bell went on to affirm that she saw her family members who were still alive when she died. This answer suggests her spirit remained in her parents' house; however, if Charles Burchett's current home is the house where Mary Bell died, why didn't she remain there instead of appearing in our house? I have two possible explanations: either Mary Bell was first buried in what is now our backyard, or she responded when we reached out to her. Since we had subtle clues that Mary Bell lived inside our home prior to our trip to the Stanley Hotel, I suspect that her original burial site was nearby.

I continued with questions regarding the dying process. Mary Bell answered positively when asked if she saw herself outside of her body after she died. This is another phenomenon associated with near-death experiences. Countless individuals who have undergone a NDE have reported that they floated out of their body and looked down at themselves and the living people who surrounded them. Mary Bell next confirmed that her relatives who had died before her were present to greet her at the time she died. While her answer conforms to reports from near-death experiences, the rods moved slowly in response to this question and barely intersected. If Mary Bell failed to cross over into the proper realm, why would she see her dead relatives? Did she start to cross, only to return to a plane closer to the living on earth? Or perhaps when people die, they all remain in a realm that is close to the living. Mary Bell next acknowledged that she remembered her own funeral. According to newspaper accounts, Mary Bell's funeral service took place in her parents' house, the location where she died. Some psychics believe that all people attend their own funerals.

I next inquired about the possible gravesite discovered in our backyard. After Duane Kniebes told us the site had been the grave of a woman who had died over one hundred years ago, I immediately suspected that the location was Mary Bell's original burial site. My reasons are as follows: 1. she died at the end of November when the ground is hard from the cold. Bodies were typically buried in shallow graves in cold-weather months because of this. 2. Mary Bell died in 1886. According to the

Harmony Cemetery records, Charles Wilson did not buy her cemetery plot until 1891. 3. Families commonly buried adults on hills, or the highest point of land. If you examine the lay of the land in our subdivision, the land crests at the spot in our backyard where we found the gravesite. 4. Charles Wilson lived with Mary Bell a half mile west of her parents' house. The gravesite in our backyard is approximately a half mile west from Charles Burchett's home, which may have belonged to the Webster family. 5. If Mary Bell was buried near our house, it explained why she haunted us. I asked Mary Bell if she had been buried in what is now our backyard, and her response was yes. Continuing with this line of inquiry, I asked Mary Bell if her body had been moved to its present location at the Harmony Cemetery and she again answered positively.

At times, we experienced a high level of anomalies. I made videos in which multiple orbs appeared at the same time. Did each sphere represent an individual spirit? When I witnessed the anomaly in our kitchen, it appeared to demonstrate intelligence. If this is true, and if each orb was an individual spirit, then who are the spirits inside our house? The first answer that comes to mind is that the entire Webster family haunted our house. I knew Mary Bell had a younger brother named Ruben who died before her. Could he be haunting our house? My youngest daughter Rebecca reported that she saw the ghost of a boy named Ruben in her bedroom, but she was very young at the time, which makes her account questionable. Rebecca had heard the name Ruben Webster prior to her experience, and knew that he was Mary Bell's brother. Did the Websters bury Mary Bell close to Ruben? Traditionally, pioneer families buried the bodies of children within view of the house. Mary Bell, however, might have been buried closer to Charles Wilson's home. When I asked Mary Bell if she had been buried near Ruben, her response was no, which made sense, but did nothing to explain the mystery of why we had so many orbs in the house.

Because Mary Bell died at her parents' house, attended her own funeral in the house, and her daughter Leona came there to live with her parents, I assumed Mary Bell's spirit stayed there. However, she answered that she did not continue to live in their house after she died. What does her answer mean? Does the spirit world overlap with our world? Do spirits move back and forth between the two realms at will? I stayed with this line of questioning and inquired if her family saw her spirit after she died. The rods responded slowly, but did eventually cross. According to my research, Mary Bell's father, Stewart Webster, developed a drinking problem around the time of her death. I wondered if his condition resulted from the presence of Mary Bell's spirit in the Webster home. I asked Mary Bell if her father started to drink after he saw her ghost, and her answer was yes. Unfortunately, Stewart Webster's alcoholism progressed to the point that his wife Margaret moved to California with Mary Bell's daughter, Leona, and none of his children wanted to be responsible for him. Eventually his son Samuel took him in. It seemed strange that a man who had worked hard his entire life, built a prosperous farm, and had no apparent history of drinking or psychological problems prior to 1886, would suddenly fall apart. The sudden loss of a daughter, and the subsequent return of her spirit, might explain why he turned to alcohol.

I next asked Mary Bell if she saw God after she died. Her positive response was in line with the answer she provided previously when I queried her if she had seen Jesus. Her answer made me wonder why a spirit stuck in the wrong plane of existence would see God. Also, you would think an angel or spirit guide would have assisted Mary Bell in crossing over when she died. When asked if she went to another place other than her family's home after her death, Mary Bell responded positively. This answer can be interpreted many ways. Does it mean she went somewhere in the spirit world, away from her family? If she stayed in the physical world, did she live in the house of her husband Charles Wilson and later move back into her parents' house when her daughter Leona came to live with them?

I next inquired as to the physical appearance of the spirit world. Mary Bell answered that it looked the same as the world of the living. Some ITC researchers have reported contacting spirits who stated that they lived in a world like the one they left behind. Do spirits cross into a separate realm or remain in ours, only traveling at a vibration that prevents us from seeing them? Perhaps the spirit world overlaps the physical world and ghosts have the ability to move within both realms. Continuing with this line of questioning, I inquired if the world in which she now lived was bright. Again, Mary Bell answered yes. There are many theories as to what awaits us in the various realms of the afterlife. Many suggest that the first realm is a place of darkness. Mark Macy, pioneering ITC researcher, calls this first realm the Quantum Realm. According to Macy, the Quantum Realm is supposed to be a gentle, relaxed area for everyone who leaves the earth; however, it has developed dismal pockets of darkness and negativity where some people get stuck for a while before moving on to the paradise of the astral worlds. Macy believes these pockets of darkness have been created mainly by humanity's spiritual ignorance, which results in a fear of death, and they have become a significant problem. They boil over and spill back on to the earth to stir up more negativity here, and they present an obstacle to many people leaving the earth and looking for paradise. If Macy's theory is correct, then Mary Bell is stuck in the Quantum Realm. However, her answer that the place where she lives is bright goes against her residing in one of the dark pockets of the Quantum Realm.

I next inquired if Mary Bell's relatives joined her where she is now after they died, and she answered no. This surprised me, because in previous communications, Mary Bell indicated that her relatives were with her. Does this answer mean she is indeed stuck in the wrong place, away from her family? I had never gotten the impression Mary Bell is not where she is supposed to be. The multiple orbs I captured on film and the ghost photograph I took in the office indicated the possibility of more than one spirit in our house. If they are not members of Mary Bell's family, who are they? I stayed with this line of inquiry and asked if she saw her relatives every day where she was now, and her answer was yes. This response was more in line with Mary Bell's previous answers.

Continuing with questions about life in the spirit world, I asked Mary Bell if she was married now. Her reply was no, which did not surprise me. Charles Wilson remarried within a couple of years after Mary Bell's death, and in a previous communication Mary Bell indicated she did not have a happy marriage with Charles. Spirits bring their personalities into the spirit world, but I wondered if spirits continued to feel emotions such as love and could fall in love with other spirits. Mary Bell answered yes. Her response made me wonder what kind of social life spirits enjoyed in the afterlife.

Whenever I used the dowsing rods, I could feel energy pulsating into my hands and arms. Sometimes this energy caused them to ache. After my extended communication on April 12, I was not able to conduct another session until the afternoon of April 14. I was able to ask Mary Bell several questions prior to stopping due to pain in my forearms. I continued with my line of inquiry regarding the emotional state of spirits and inquired if spirits could fall in love with the living. I was not surprised when she answered yes. Spirits see us on a daily basis and they retain their personalities, and their ability to reason, so it made sense they could feel love, even for someone who is not living in their realm. While this answer touched on the relationship between spirits and the living within our plane, I wondered about the relationship between spirits in their realm. Did spirits marry other spirits the way people married here on Earth? I posed this question to Mary Bell, and her answer was no.

Mary Bell had answered that spirits could fall in love with each other and with living persons. What would these relationships be like in her world? I decided to inquire if spirits could have sexual relations with other spirits. Mary Bell's response was no, which did not surprise me, since the purpose of sex is the reproduction of the species, and why would spirits need to reproduce? Mary

Bell's answer, while no doubt disappointing to some, confirms reports from psychics such as Sylvia Browne, who state that spirits are not capable of having sex, but are able to join in a manner that is even better than sex. We can only hope.

Based on earlier examinations, I knew Mary Bell was capable of watching my family as we went about our business. I assumed she stayed with us most of the time, and observed us every day. However, when I questioned her if she saw the people in my family every day, her answer came back as no. Her response surprised me, but I also found comfort in it, for I had always hoped that she had better things to do with her time than watch us. Of course, her answer indicated that she visited locations outside our home, which made me wonder if she lived in houses besides ours. Did Mary Bell also watch our neighbors? I inquired if she lived in a house other than ours and Mary Bell answered no. If she only lived in our house, but traveled to different places, where did she go?

Wanting to learn more about the world Mary Bell inhabits, I inquired if the buildings in her world appeared the same as they do in our world. Mary Bell responded yes. According to Mark Macy, ITC researchers have communicated with spirits whose testimony suggested they live in a place that resembles the physical world. One of the spirits was a Native American who described living in the same village he grew up in, while the spirit of an Arab merchant described his world as being an ancient market filled with activity and commerce. So, if Mary Bell still saw the world in the same way she did while physically alive, would she recognize Fort Collins as her home? Mary Bell responded that she still lived in Fort Collins. Did this mean Mary Bell remained in the physical world, only moving at a higher vibration that prevented us from seeing her, or did she live in a world that never changes? If a spirit traveled into different realms as some suggest, why would she still identify Fort Collins as her home?

About this time, my stomach growled, which led me to my next question. Do you still eat food where you are now? Mary Bell's positive response surprised me. A living person needs food for energy, but why would a spirit need food? Perhaps she is referring to energy that ghosts must absorb in order to manifest. Staying with this line of questions, I queried if she still drank where she is now and once more, her answer was yes. According to medium Andy Ford, a spirit's surroundings will be as familiar to them as the one left behind until they decide they no longer need this comfort. This includes continuing to eat and drink or even sleep until becoming accustomed to their new environments. If spirits ate and drank, did they also have some form of entertainment? I asked Mary Bell if she had entertainment where she is now, and her response was yes. The rods responded slowly to this question, and crossed only at the tips. In many near-death experiences, the person reported seeing spirits playing music. If spirits live in communities, it only makes sense that they would have entertainment.

When asked if she read books in the spirit world, Mary Bell answered yes. Her reply made me wonder if writers continued to create books in the afterlife. A woman from England named Stella Horrocks believes they continue to pursue their craft after they have died. Horrocks, a retired schoolteacher, claims that some of the world's greatest authors including Virginia Woolf, Thomas Hardy, Charles Dickens, and Jane Austen have dictated new works through her. Horrocks has created letters, speeches, diaries, memoirs, plays, and books through automatic writing and each has been in a different handwriting. Horrocks claims she can recognize the individual characteristics of each of her authors. Her technique for "tuning in" to dead authors is to let them contact her when they are ready. She said that her mind must be a complete blank in order to receive. Those who practice automatic writing sincerely believe they are in touch with the spirits of writers of the past who are anxious to prove that life continues beyond the grave.

Since Mary Bell died before the invention of motion pictures, I doubted that she watched movies; however, if she remained within our plane of existence, it is entirely possible she has kept up with changes in technology, and perhaps takes advantage of them. I next inquired if she watched movies where she was now, and Mary Bell answered yes. Somewhat surprised by her answer, I decided to purse this inquiry to learn if she interacted with other spirits while doing this. I asked her if she watched movies with her family, and she said no.

I had not been able to determine the extent of Mary Bell's relationship with her family in the afterlife. She reported seeing them on a daily basis, and we had reason to believe that more than one spirit visited our house, but this answer indicated she does not always socialize with them. I went on to ask if she listened to music in the spirit world and Mary answered yes. Some people who have undergone near-death experiences reported hearing beautiful music that surrounds them. They described the sound as modern New Age music. Around our house, Mary Bell gets a heavy dose of rock and roll.

Having established that Mary Bell enjoys various forms of entertainment in the spirit world, I wondered if spirits maintained certain traditions, such as holiday celebrations. Mary Bell said that she did not celebrate holidays. This response surprised me. I assumed if a spirit took their personality and memories with them into the afterlife, they would also bring customs such as holiday celebrations. I had posed this question previously with the same result. Because Mary Bell had previously stated that she saw both God and Jesus in the afterlife, I definitely thought that spirits might continue to celebrate Christmas and Easter in honor of Christ.

I moved in a different direction with the next question. The subject of orbs is controversial among paranormal investigators. Some dismiss them outright because cameras, particularly digital cameras, sometimes produce false orbs. However, based on my investigation, and the evidence obtained in photographs and video, plus having actually seen an orb with my eyes, I knew that some orbs were in fact paranormal in nature, a position supported by longtime ghost hunter Troy Taylor. Still, I wanted to confirm with Mary Bell that she moved about in the form of a ball of bright light, so I asked if she did this. Mary Bell answered yes—the rods reacted quickly to this question. Why do ghosts use this form? According to ghoststudy.com, ghosts prefer the orb form because it takes less energy. If ghosts travel around in the shape of spheres, is that how they see each other? Mary Bell said no.

I've always suspected that spirits see other spirits in human form. Whenever a person has a near-death experience in which they see deceased relatives, they describe them as looking the way they did while alive. When I asked Mary Bell to appear to us in human form, she absorbed energy for several days in order to appear, as she would have while alive, complete with dress. To expand upon this idea, I questioned Mary Bell if her family appeared to her in the same way they looked while they were alive, and she answered yes.

I started to wonder if spirits remain fixed to a single location, or to a town, or if they traveled to other places. Mary Bell said she traveled outside of Fort Collins. This did not explain where or how Mary Bell traveled, but it did raise the possibility that spirits traveled from the location they populated in the physical world, something I was to find out for myself later on. Mary Bell then confirmed that there were many spirits living where she is; however, I felt a great deal of hesitancy in the rods after I posed this question, and they barely crossed at the tips.

My next question is the one that probably keeps more than a few people up at night with worry: Is there a hell? Unfortunately for all of us sinners, Mary Bell answered yes. In fact, the rods moved quickly in response to this question. I do wonder how she knows that hell exists. Has she actually seen it? If so, why would she have seen it? Having established the existence of hell, I next inquired about heaven. Mary Bell confirmed that heaven is real, and once more, the rods responded quickly. Since the majority of paranormal investigators consider ghosts to be spirits that failed to cross over to the proper realm, I asked Mary Bell if she was in the place she was supposed to be. She affirmed that she was in the proper place. Mary Bell had never given me any reason to believe she is in the wrong location or stuck in the wrong realm. However, she does fit the classic profile of a ghost that did not cross over. She died at a young age. Due to the nature of her illness, she would not have been aware of her pending death. She left behind a young child. She remains tied to the land that her family farmed while she was alive.

During my investigation, my family came to believe that we established a relationship with Mary Bell. In a strange way, she became a part of our family. With this in mind, I wondered if Mary Bell would follow us if we ever moved. I asked her this, and her response was no. However, when we did move out of the house, we had experiences that led us to believe Mary Bell may have followed us, or possibly visited. Dominick Villella from Paranormal Investigation of New York believes paranormal activity is confined to a certain location: "I don't think it is possible to move any type of paranormal activity from one building to the next." Others insist that ghosts can attach themselves to individuals or objects as well as locations. I followed this question by asking Mary Bell if we could still communicate with her if we moved, and she answered yes. I could see no reason why we should not be able to continue communicating with Mary Bell. However, I do not believe it would be as easy to make a connection if we lived somewhere else. Once we did establish a connection with Mary Bell, and if we reached out to her on a daily basis, I am sure the spirit activity would increase in our new home. But would we want this to happen?

My next communication with Mary Bell took place on April 15, at 11:30 a.m. I was able to make an immediate connection with her and opened by inquiring if she needed to absorb energy, such as electricity from a video camera battery in order to appear in human form. Although this was a confusing question, Mary Bell answered yes without hesitation. Her response did not surprise me since I had collected evidence that proved she drew energy from electrical devices prior to manifesting. Not only had I captured this phenomenon on video, it had been witnessed by several members of my family.

I changed course with the next question and asked if she stayed in the same place where she had lived when she died. Her answer was yes. If Mary Bell is in the proper realm, and not stuck in the wrong place, this answer would seem to confirm my suspicion that when we die we simply leave our bodies and stay in the same location. Although many people accept there are multiple layers or realms within the universe, until we have the technology to breach these layers, I will continue to believe spirits share the same plane as the living.

After Mary Bell responded to my telepathic requests to appear in human form, I wondered if she controlled when and where this would happen. Not only did she appear in human form after my requests back in September

2007, she also appeared in front of Sarah in December after I asked her to. Based on this, it did not surprise me when she confirmed that she picked when and where she would appear. However, I also maintain that spirits sometimes appear by accident. This would explain why both Monika and Sarah spotted Mary Bell moving in the hallway toward the kids' room. In addition, one night around 9:00 p.m., I was on the phone with my brother when I witnessed shimmering silver light slice through the air in front of me several times. This light moved about the family room, appearing at various heights. I believe the light was Mary Bell penetrating the barrier that separates our worlds without fully crossing over.

Because I had experienced the feeling that a spirit attempted to talk to me for several nights in a row prior to my visit to the Fort Collins Museum, I wondered if Mary Bell communicated to us while we slept. Mary Bell said yes. Famous psychic Edgar Cayce believed that spirits communicate with us while we are sleeping:

> *During the dreaming state of sleep, we experience the different levels of consciousness and receive input from the different realms of the spirit world. All subconscious minds are in contact with one another. Through the subconscious, dreams may place us in attunement with those in the physical realm or those in the spiritual realm. We may be visited in the night by*

> *discarnate entities for many reasons; they may seek to give us assurance about their well-being in other realms of existence; they may come seeking our aid through prayer; they may come to bring us information which may be very helpful or limited; or they may come to influence us with their own desires or perspectives, which may be helpful or harmful. The dead differ from the living only in this respect: they are in a permanently subconscious state because the conscious mind of the physical body no longer exists. But the body is an expendable shell, and all else is intact. On the astral level of existence, the subconscious mind replaces the conscious mind of the soul, and the superconscious replaces the subconscious. Hence, in dream, we find that communication with those who have passed on is more logical than the average person is able to comprehend.*

Many people believe that our souls leave the body while we are sleeping. On several occasions when Mary Bell communicated with me as I slept, I thought I had left my body. I asked Mary Bell if our souls left the body while we slept, and she answered yes. Psychic Sylvia Browne claims that when our bodies are resting, our soul leaves and travels through many different dimensions. Browne states that people who suffer paralysis at the time they awaken are experiencing the return of the soul into their bodies. Symptoms include hearing a loud noise like rushing wind, a feeling of being held down, trying to yell without making a sound. Browne says this occurs because our conscious mind becomes aware of our spirit either returning or leaving the body and panics, causing us to have what Browne calls Astral Catalepsy. When I was a teenager, I often experienced the symptoms described by Browne. These experiences were terrifying and made me afraid to go to sleep. Since Mary Bell affirmed that *my spirit* wandered at night, I inquired if my spirit visited her while I slept, and she answered that it did. I next asked her if she visited with the spirits of my family members while they slept, and again she said yes. Her answer made me wonder why they never had the sensation of Mary Bell visiting them during the night. I can only assume that during the times I remembered her visiting me, I was not in a deep level of sleep. Mary Bell confirmed that she visited with our spirits every night while we slept. This answer supports my theory that spirits are more active at night because spirits of the living range outside their bodies while they sleep, which makes it easier for the dead to communicate with us.

Because I twice had dreams that featured deceased family pets, I wondered if the spirits of animals lived where Mary Bell was. Her response was yes, which did not surprise me since the Book of Revelation discusses animals in heaven. To be more specific with my next question, I inquired if the spirit of my dog Jeff was living where Mary Bell is, and again her response was positive.

Both Monika and I have experienced hearing voices inside our house, so I asked Mary Bell if it was possible for us to hear her voice while we were awake, and she affirmed that it was possible. When we first became aware of Mary Bell's presence, we attempted to record her voice. On at least two occasions, I heard a voice on the video responding to my questions.

My next question involved my failed ITC experiment. I wanted to know if Mary Bell could appear on my television, and she confirmed that it was possible. I then inquired if she would allow me to see her on our television, and her response was no. I believe Mary Bell is embarrassed to let me see her because I am the only male in the house. Not only did she refuse to let me see her on the TV, she would not manifest in my presence despite my requests to let me see her in human form. Mary Bell did say that she could contact us by calling on the telephone. According to Mark Macy and other ITC researchers, spirits have the ability to call the living. There have been numerous incidents were people have reported being contacted by deceased persons on the telephone. The majority of these ghost calls take place on days of importance such as Mother's Day or birthdays. The telephone rings normally but the connection is usually bad with static. The voice of the deceased tends to grow fainter as the call progresses. Sometimes the voice fades away completely. In some cases, the call is placed long distance and connected by an operator; however, checks with the telephone company turn up no evidence of a call. Phone calls are sometimes placed to the dead as well. A person places a call to someone only to find out later that the person was dead at the time. To my knowledge, Mary Bell has never tried to call us, although Monika's cell phone did call mine several times on its own.

Mary Bell demonstrated the ability to touch objects in our house. She threw pictures off the wall and knocked on doors and our headboard. In addition, she seemed to enjoy touching my arm and toes while I was in bed. I wondered if she could feel the objects she touched. Mary Bell confirmed that she could feel these objects. To further verify her capabilities, I inquired if she could lift and move objects, and Mary Bell answered yes. How does she do it? My guess is she uses the power of her mind through telekinesis to move objects. In addition to tossing the pictures, Mary Bell caused a music box to play and knocked the telephone receiver from its cradle.

I next asked Mary Bell about spirit communication. Mary Bell confirmed that she used her mouth to talk with other spirits, and not her mind. It makes more sense to me that spirits would use telepathy, as reported by people who have gone through near-death experiences. In our world, we speak to each other verbally and to spirits using telepathy. Perhaps it is the same in the spirit world, where they communicate to each other by voice, and to the living through telepathy.

I next went on to establish that Mary Bell could see me as I asked her questions. On the day I started to communicate with Mary Bell using the rods, she demonstrated that she saw us in real time by identifying the color of our clothes and the people in a room by name. I wondered if spirits had the ability to create things in their realm. Mary Bell confirmed that she could do this.

Many researchers theorize that the dying process is similar to being born, except when we are born, we have no prior memories or education, while spirits take these with them into the afterlife. I asked Mary Bell if she was reborn after her death, and she answered yes. She went on to say that spirits do not grow old. Some paranormal investigators and psychics believe spirits never age and take on the appearance of the deceased person when they were in the prime of their lives (between ages twenty-five and thirty-five). Continuing with this line of questions, I inquired if spirits could die. Her answer was no. Some researchers have suggested that when people die, they become spirits for a short period and then the spirit dies. Mary Bell then went on to say spirits live forever—considering that she has been around since 1886, it does not appear spirits die soon after entering the spirit world. I next inquired if spirits are reborn on earth into new bodies. Mary Bell quickly answered no. While her response would appear to dismiss the possibility of reincarnation, some psychics suggest that spirits have the option of reincarnation. If Mary Bell is stuck in the wrong realm, she may not have been given that option.

I next queried about the physical makeup of the spirit world. The first thing I asked her was if there are streets in the spirit world. Mary Bell answered yes. Although I sensed hesitation in the rods at first, once Mary Bell responded, the rods crossed quickly. If spirits continue to live alongside the living, they would be exposed to advances in technology, including cars. To test this theory, I inquired if there were cars in the spirit world. Mary Bell confirmed that there were cars. She went on to say that she saw buildings in the spirit world. I expanded upon this to find out if Mary Bell views the same buildings we do. Her answer was yes, which makes sense if she is stuck in the world of the living, but what about spirits who have crossed over. Did they leave this realm or remain here with us? Perhaps spirits can cross back and forth between the two planes of existence. Mary Bell confirmed that she continued to live around her family after she died. This answer can be interpreted two ways: either Mary Bell is stuck between worlds and stayed close to her family while they were alive, but is no longer living with them, or she is in the right place and they live there with her. Mary Bell said she was present when members of her family died and crossed over into the spirit world, which supports the eyewitness accounts from doctors and nurses who have reported seeing the dead relatives of patients who were near death. Right before my Uncle Jay died, his eyes widened and he stared up into one corner of the hospital room in a trance as if watching something or someone. Did he see my late grandfather and grandmother waiting to welcome him into his new life? I next inquired if she was happy where she is now, and her answer was yes. Mary Bell has never given us a reason to believe she is unhappy. She certainly did not fit the description of a sad, wailing ghost. And while we often sense her presence, she is not always with us. There have been times when I filmed in the kitchen or upstairs and did not record a single orb.

After I finished this communication, I discovered that a ghost-hunting group based in Denver had sent me an email regarding a future event at the Lumber Baron Inn in Denver. While going online to research the inn, I found a website that described a ghost as the spirit of someone who had died but did not realize it, which caused the spirit to stay in the place where he or she died instead of crossing over to the proper realm. Whenever I had communicated with Mary Bell, she never gave me the impression that she was in the wrong place, but I decided to find out if she knew that she was dead. Mary

Bell answered yes. The rods moved quickly with no hesitation, which leads me to believe that Mary Bell understands she is dead. When I previously inquired if she was in the proper place, her answer was yes.

I conducted the next communication the following afternoon. I began with questions to verify that she saw me in real time and could identify me by name. I first attempted to trick her by asking if my name is Bob, and then John, but she correctly identified my name as Ken. She was then able to identify the color of the shirt I was wearing. I gave her the wrong color twice in an attempt to fool her, and once again, she gave me the correct answer: white. I had never been able to trick Mary Bell, so I planned to mix things up a little. Whenever I had tried a trick question, I always stated the trick question first. I wondered how Mary Bell would answer if after correctly identifying the color of my pants, I tried the question again, only this time using the wrong color. After correctly answering that my pants were blue, I tried to fool her twice, but to no avail. She then went on to correctly identify my wife as Monika and my ex wife as Dana.

I next tested Mary Bell's knowledge of my family. She was able to identify one of my grandfathers as Loren and that he was born in Kansas. I asked Mary Bell if she knew information about my family because she had heard us talking about them, but she answered no. It was becoming clear that Mary Bell displayed clairvoyance, which enabled her to know details about my family's past. I had tried to ask her questions regarding future events, but her answers proved inaccurate. This led me to believe that spirits cannot see into the future.

Some psychics claim that spirits can travel back in time. Mary Bell answered that she could do this. There are many schools of thought regarding the possibility of time travel. The relativity of simultaneity in modern physics favors the philosophic view known as four dimensionalism in which past, present, and future events all coexist in a single space-time. Block Universe theory, or eternalism, builds on a standard method of modeling time as a dimension in physics, to give time a similar ontology to that of space. This would mean that time is just another dimension, that future events are "already there," and that there is no objective flow of time. Presentism is a school of philosophy that holds that neither the future nor the past exist, and there are no non-present objects. In this view, time travel is impossible because there is no future or past. According to Dr. Bob Gibson, time travel is an ability shared by all spirits, "Another ability that takes getting used to is travel. In spirit form, we experience a much higher energy mode than on the earth plane. Science has shown that higher energy levels do funny things to time and space. For spirits, time does some telescoping, meaning that days, months, and years seem to overlap to some degree. This higher energy mode allows travel to be almost instantaneous, almost as soon as you think of where you want to go, you are there."

Since Mary Bell had said she could travel back in time, I wondered if she traveled back to the time when she was alive, and she answered yes. It made sense that Mary Bell would travel back in time to a period familiar to her. But why would she go back in time? Some experts believe spirits can travel immediately back to the source of any question, so answers can be found to anything by going to the time of the event in question. Thus time traveling is one of the favorite pastimes of spirits. If this were true, it would explain how Mary Bell could answer questions regarding my family and historical events. I asked Mary Bell if she traveled back to a period prior to her birth, and her answer was yes. I can imagine how much fun a history buff could have bouncing between centuries to witness historical events. Where would you go? I have always enjoyed Civil War history, so I can see myself going back to Gettysburg, but the first place I would go to is Bethlehem to witness the birth of Jesus Christ.

Having established that Mary Bell had traveled back in time, I wondered if she also traveled into the future. Mary Bell confirmed that she did. I wasn't surprised that she had the ability, but why would she want to? She went on to affirm she had traveled more than five hundred years into the future. I was tempted to ask her if life on Earth was going to end in 2012, as some predict based on the Mayan calendar, but Sarah did not want me to pursue this line of questioning, so this will have to remain a mystery. Since Mary Bell indicated she travels in time, I wondered if spirits kept track of time. I inquired if she did this where she is now, and her answer was yes. Most mediums and spiritualists believe there is no sense of time passing within the spirit world. Mary Bell's answer would appear to make sense only if she shared the same realm as the living or is stuck in the wrong realm. Regardless of her current location, when I asked if she was happier now than when she was alive, her answer was yes. We all would like to go to a better place when we die, so I found this answer comforting. This statement also reaffirms the reports from near-death experiences in which the dying person remembers not wanting to return to their body because they were happier in the spirit world.

I returned to a line of questioning that explored her life within the spirit world. Some of Mary Bell's answers indicated she lived in the same realm as the living, which means either she is stuck in the wrong plane, or all spirits share the same plane with the living. Mary Bell answered yes when I asked her if she sometimes traveled by car. I could not figure out why a spirit would need a car, but later discovered she sometimes accompanied us on trips. Mary Bell answered no when I inquired if she ever traveled by airplane. Her response was not a surprise, but I did wonder if she would join us on an airplane if we took a flight. I decided to gauge the level of interaction between spirits and the living. Do they socialize in the same places we do? Since Mary Bell previously indicated that she watched movies, is it possible she watched them inside movie theaters with the living? Mary Bell responded yes to this question. Again, since movies had not been invented when Mary Bell died, this answer suggested that spirits remain aware of changes in human technology. One person undergoing a near-death experience reported seeing Albert Einstein using a computer. I expanded my inquiry to learn if other spirits also watched movies in theaters with the living, and again, Mary Bell answered yes. For several years after we moved into our house, Mary Bell only provided subtle hints of her existence, but once we reached out to her, especially after I began using telepathy to communicate, the level of interaction between Mary Bell and us increased dramatically. Is it common for spirits to try to have a relationship with the living? I inquired if spirits interact with the living all the time and she answered yes. I believe all spirits, whether stuck in this realm as ghosts or having crossed over, can interact with the living. It would seem that spirits who have crossed are more likely to contact the living in dreams, rather than manifest in front of them.

How much does the spirit world mirror our own? I asked Mary Bell if spirits had jobs, and she confirmed this. Some ITC researchers have reported contacting spirits who lived and worked in environments that resembled their lives on earth. If this is true, it suggests that our lives in the spirit world continue in much the same way. When questioned if they used money in the spirit world, Mary Bell responded no. This makes sense. Then again, why would they continue to have jobs? Perhaps Mary Bell is implying that spirits do the things they loved to do while alive. I like to write; maybe I will continue to write in the afterlife. Religion plays an important role in the lives of many people—does this continue after we have died? According to Mary Bell, spirits still worship God. This answer did not surprise me, since she already answered that she has seen both God and Jesus.

Most of us think of the spirit world as a peaceful place, free from the horrors of war. I asked Mary Bell if there were, in fact, wars in the spirit world. To my relief, her answer was no. This did not surprise me because I cannot imagine why spirits would fight. Does Mary Bell keep up with the events that are happening in our world? I asked if she was aware of wars occurring on earth, and she answered yes. If spirits share our world, it is no surprise they would know what is happening in it. However, I have read accounts of near-death experiences in which spirits indicated they did not keep up with what was happening on earth. Mary Bell previously answered that she lived in Fort Collins, but does she recognize the country in which she resides? I asked Mary Bell what country she lived in. I first tried to trick her by questioning if she lived in Canada, but this did not fool her. I then inquired if she lived in the United States of America, but Mary Bell answered no. She correctly identified the town she was in, but not the country. What did this mean?

Since Mary Bell did not recognize the United States of America as the country where she resided, I wondered if she was aware of current events involving the U. S. government. I asked her if the United States was engaged in a war, and she replied yes. This response made no sense considering Mary Bell's response to the last question. Why would she be aware of the existence of the United States, but not identify it as her home? Perhaps in the spirit world they do not align themselves with a particular country, which would explain the absence of government and wars. Since Mary Bell correctly answered that the United States was at war, I probed to learn if she knew whom we were fighting. I once again tried to trick her by asking if the United States was fighting a war with England, but she said no. But she correctly answered when asked if we were fighting a war in Iraq. How is she aware of current events? Do spirits get their news from watching television or from hearing the living discuss what is happening in the world?

After my failed ITC experiment with Mary Bell, I wondered if I would have more luck attempting to contact the spirit of someone I knew such as my grandmother,

Ollie Harmon. According to Mary Bell, it is possible for me to contact the spirit of my grandmother. Hearing this, I wanted to try to communicate with my grandmother. But how to do it? Would the dowsing rods work for someone who died and is buried in another state? I inquired if I should try to have my grandmother appear on my television. Mary Bell answered yes. Mary Bell told me that ITC works; however, she would not allow me to see her on the television. Perhaps I would have more luck with a spirit who knew me. I next inquired if spirits communicated with the living in order to give them advice, and Mary Bell responded yes. No surprise here, people have reported receiving advice from spirits for hundreds of years. Edgar Cayce believed that spirits provided information to the living while they slept. My final question for Mary Bell was if there are people or creatures alive on planets other than Earth. She answered no. Her response puzzled me because when I inquired about UFOs, Mary Bell indicated that aliens were real. I wonder if Mary Bell had difficulty understanding the question because it was difficult to word, or perhaps aliens do not live on planets in our plane of existence, but in parallel universes, and move between the two.

Chapter Fifteen

I experienced many strange events while living with the spirit of Mary Bell Wilson. One of the strangest occurred on my forty-seventh birthday. The day started normally. Monika made me breakfast in bed and the kids greeted me with happy birthday wishes. Around one in the afternoon, I felt unusually tired and opted to take a nap upstairs in the master bedroom before we went to my parents' house. When I first laid down, Amanda and Rebecca kept coming into the room, which kept me awake. At some point, I drifted into a deep sleep.

The next thing I knew, I was standing beside the bed. I had no memory of waking or getting off the bed. I glanced around the bright room. Everything appeared as it always did and I knew that it was the afternoon of my birthday. I started to move toward the closed bedroom door but did not feel my feet touching the floor. When I reached the master bedroom closet, it swung open. I peered into the empty closet and immediately thought of Mary Bell. I next found myself standing in front of the closed bedroom door. I grabbed the doorknob and tried to pull the door open, but someone was pulling from the other side, which prevented me from leaving the room. Suddenly, I was back on the bed, covered with a sheet. I had no memory of returning to the bed. One second I was struggling to open the door and the next I was on the bed. My eyes were closed and my head felt heavy. I struggled to open my eyes but found it impossible. I finally resorted to reaching up with my right hand and prying my right eyelid open. Once I was able to see the room and focus on my surroundings, I could open my left eye. Immediately, I sensed that I had undergone an out-of-body experience. The event did not feel like a dream. My dreams are typically short and not at all vivid. During this incident, not only could I see my surroundings as if I were awake, but I also knew the date and time of day.

As I tried to make sense of what happened, it occurred to me that Mary Bell had saved me from serious mental or even physical injury. If I was in fact outside of my body and had been able to leave the bedroom and approach my family, I might have attempted to communicate with them. When they failed to answer me, I may have realized that I was outside my body. I am sure that panic would have set in. What would have happened if I could not find my way back to my body or if the shock of realizing that I was outside of my body caused me to have a heart attack?

I came to believe that Mary Bell saw my spirit ranging outside of my body and reacted to stop me from seeing my family while in this state. She did this by opening the closet door to distract me and then holding the bedroom door closed to prevent my exit. If this was true, why could I not see Mary Bell? Perhaps the spirit of a living person and that of someone deceased moved at a different frequency.

To confirm what had happened, I contacted Mary Bell with the dowsing rods. I asked her if my spirit had traveled outside my body, and she said yes. I then asked if she had opened the closet door, and again she answered yes. She also confirmed that she had prevented me from leaving the room by holding the door closed to keep me from seeing my family while in this condition. I thanked Mary Bell for saving me from an uncertain fate. If my spirit had in fact left my body, then spirits view their surroundings with total clarity and complete awareness.

In the summer of 2008, two of Monika's sisters visited from Europe with their families. I had met her sister Henny once, eight years earlier when I married Monika, along with Stanis, the husband of her sister Hetty, who also was coming. As their visit neared, I felt apprehensive, but once they arrived, my nerves calmed. Henny and Hetty were both quiet and friendly and I soon felt at ease around them and their families. Playing the role of good host, I had to help come up with ways to entertain them. We decided to drive to Denver. I suggested we visit the Molly Brown house. I figured they had heard of the legendary heiress who survived the sinking of the Titanic, and my family had always wanted to visit the house.

Tall trees with heavy foliage hide the Molly Brown house from the road. We may never have found it if not for the red, white, and blue bunting that decorated the front. Prior to leaving Fort Collins, we called for tour information and learned that the Molly Brown Society was celebrating her birthday today. Architect William A. Lang built the house, located at 1340 Pennsylvania Street, in the 1880s. He incorporated several popular styles from that era, including the Queen Anne style for the original owners, Isaac and Mary Large. Molly Brown's husband James Joseph Brown purchased the home in 1894.

At the start of the tour, we were crowded into the entry to listen to a snooty young woman who was to act as our guide. She gave a brief overview of the house's history and then reminded everyone that smoking and photography were not permitted. The photography ban was a disappointment. I had heard that the house was haunted and wanted to take a few pictures to see if anything turned up. We followed the guide through the rooms of the house, her ever-vigilant eyes boring into us. I would have enjoyed the tour better if she had not herded us along like cattle. When you have thirty people in a small space on a hot summer day, the atmosphere can become unpleasant in a hurry. I managed to snap off one photograph when the group started up the stairs to the second floor. After the guide told us the history of the upstairs bedrooms, I lingered behind as the group headed toward the kitchen, hoping to take another picture. Unfortunately, a couple and the scowling tour guide stayed behind with me. As I gazed into Molly Brown's bedroom, I suddenly smelled cigar smoke. The odor was strong and unmistakable. I wondered where the smell came from. Unable to take another photograph, I tramped downstairs into the small kitchen and rejoined my family.

After leaving the Molly Brown house, we walked to the Cathedral Basilica of the Immaculate Conception. This stunning cathedral, consecrated in 1921 and inspired by French Gothic architecture, is 195 feet by 116 feet with a vaulted ceiling rising 68 feet above the sloping nave. The exterior was made of limestone from Indiana and granite from Colorado. The altar, statuary, and bishop's chair are all made of marble imported from Carrara, Italy. The seventy-five stained-glass windows came from the F. X. Zetter's Royal Bavarian Institute of Munich and are considered among the finest in the world. We paused for a few minutes inside the church to escape the heat.

We ended the day eating at a Black Eyed Pea Restaurant. For Monika's family, accustomed to European food, eating chicken-fried steaks proved a memorable experience. After we got back to Fort Collins, we dropped Monika's relatives off at the hotel. Stanis and Henny's husband Albert followed us home to drop off some suitcases. They were going to Las Vegas for a week, so we offered to let them leave bags in our garage. After they left, I jumped on the Internet to do research on the Molly Brown house. I wondered if anyone else had reported smelling cigar smoke. I learned that the house has a history of paranormal activity with many guests and employees smelling the scent of James Joseph Brown's cigars.

I used the dowsing rods to contact Mary Bell. I wanted to ask if she could identify the two men who had dropped off luggage at our house. To my surprise, she not only identified both Stanis and Albert by name, despite my attempt to trick her, but also identified the countries where they lived. When you think of ghosts, you tend to think of them staying in one place, but I knew from earlier questioning that Mary Bell traveled. I wondered if she had gone to Denver with us. I started by asking Mary Bell to identify the people who rode in our van on the trip to Denver. Mary Bell correctly identified every passenger. I asked Mary Bell if she visited the Molly Brown house, and she said yes. I then inquired if the ghosts of Molly Brown and James Brown were present inside the house, and again Mary Bell answered yes. I next asked if we had visited another building after leaving the Molly Brown house, and again, Mary Bell gave the correct answer. I tried to trick her by providing false information about the type of building we visited, but Mary Bell did not respond until I used the word "church." After further questioning, she went on to correctly identify the name of the restaurant, the people who sat next to me inside the restaurant, and what we ate for dinner.

My sister Debbie and her daughter Kimberly came to visit a few days later. One evening, we entertained them at our house. After we watched some of the video evidence I had collected, I showed them how to use the dowsing rods to communicate with Mary Bell. Both of them were able to use the rods to communicate with her. While my sister talked with Mary Bell, she asked if Kimberly had ever driven while intoxicated. Mary Bell answered yes. An agitated Kimberly told us that she had never driven while drunk in her life and Mary Bell was wrong. Later, Kimberly was telling us about her experience playing golf with some of her friends. She said they played a game in which everyone took their shot from a tee, and then all ran to the ball hit closest to the flag. Kimberly went on to say the game was more fun if everyone was drunk. She paused and then said, "You know what, I drove the golf cart while I was drunk." Once again, Mary Bell knew an answer that she should not have known.

When I prepared to drive my sister and niece to my parents' house, I tried an experiment. I contacted Mary Bell using the dowsing rods and invited her to go with us. After we got in the car, I turned to my sister and told her to say the first country that came to mind. At first, Debbie appeared confused, but once she realized what I was doing, she said Australia. After dropping them off, I returned home and used the rods to contact Mary Bell. I asked if she rode with us when I dropped Debbie and Kimberly off. Her answer was yes. I then inquired if she heard Debbie say the name of a country. Again, her answer was yes. I named several wrong countries to trick Mary Bell, but she did not respond. When I said Australia, the rods crossed to indicate a positive response.

After this, I took time off from my investigation. I needed a rest from the daily grind of communicating and gathering evidence. Although I stopped reaching out to Mary Bell on a daily basis, she still found ways to let us know she was with us. She frequently knocked on doors. One night in the master bedroom, right after I climbed in bed, Mary Bell knocked three times on our elliptical machine. We often saw flashes of light or shadow moving through the air around us. One night in the family room, I was sitting on the couch watching TV when a cold spot appeared in front of me from my mid-thigh forward. The air felt freezing cold and stayed this way for more than one minute.

I did attempt one more experiment with Mary Bell. On several occasions, I had one of my daughters pose for a photograph and asked Mary Bell telepathically if she would allow me to take her picture with my daughter. Every time, an orb appeared in the photograph next to the girl. On March 9, 2009, I tried this experiment using the video camera. At about 10:30 p.m., filming in the dark using nightshot, I had Michelle stand in front of the artificial tree in the family room. I then contacted Mary Bell telepathically to see if I could take her picture with Michelle. Almost immediately a white object that resembled a small cloud appeared. It rushed down from the ceiling, passed Michelle, turned and spun around, headed away from her, spun a second time, and then flew off toward the ceiling. What surprised me about this video is not only did Mary Bell appear when requested, but also the white object was not an orb as I expected. Comparing its size against Michelle, I would say the object is between six and eight inches tall. I tried to repeat this experiment a week later with my daughter Amanda, but she would not stay near the tree long enough for me to film her. At one point, while she was sitting on the couch watching TV, I asked Mary Bell if I could take her picture with Amanda, and a low orb appeared near the couch.

I filmed off and on in the family room for two months. During this time, I captured some incredible images. One night as I turned on the video camera, I said to Michelle, "I don't expect Mary Bell to show up tonight." Suddenly orbs started to fly all over the room. I counted ten in the first ten seconds. On another tape, the girls were standing in front of the artificial tree singing a special song they had made up for Mary Bell, when a small white cloud appeared in front of them. It climbed toward the ceiling using a swimming motion, vanished briefly, and then came fluttering down in front of the fireplace. The strange thing about this image was that the object appeared more solid than the one from March 9, and seemed to have a tail. A few weeks later as I filmed in the same location, two orbs appeared. As they zigzagged across the room, I shouted, "Look at that!" Later, as I watched the tape, I noticed that something strange occurred when I shouted. A solid black image flew into view over our TV, spun about, and quickly flew out of sight. I had never filmed anything like it before. How did this black object appear while I filmed in the dark with no backlighting? I contacted Mary Bell with the dowsing rods and inquired if she was the black object. Her answer was no. I then questioned her if the black object represented something evil and again her answer was no.

After this, I considered launching a new investigation but elected not to. While I wanted to collect further evidence, I just was not ready to invest the time and energy required.

Chapter Sixteen

In February of 2010, our landlord informed us that he needed to sell the house. We quickly found a new home to rent and started to pack. It felt strange to be leaving the place we had called home for nearly six years, and it felt strange to be leaving Mary Bell. At the start of the year, I had joined a second writer's group. One of the group members, April Moore, inquired about Mary Bell after having read about her in the bio I posted on the group's website. After I told her the story, I asked April if she wanted to come to the house with her husband, Curt, and twelve-year-old son, Connor, and attempt to hold a communication. April told me that Connor was crazy about ghosts and watched all the ghost hunting shows on TV, so they would be delighted to visit. By the time they came to the house, we had moved almost all of the furniture. We gathered behind a table in the kitchen and turned out the lights. Prior to their arrival, I had played religious hymns on my iPod. We communicated with Mary Bell for thirty minutes without recording any activity on our video cameras. Connor then stepped out in front of the table and started to ask Mary Bell questions. Finally, after several minutes of this, a single orb appeared. I suggested we move into the family room and try again. Once again, Connor stepped out in front of the camera, only this time, an orb flashed past him almost immediately. Over the next twenty minutes, five orbs appeared around Connor.

On our last day in the house, I stood for a long time in the kitchen and stared at the empty family room. I wondered if Mary Bell would make her presence known to the next family who lived in the house. To my surprise, Mary Bell did make her presence known, but not in the location I had expected.

Right after we moved into the new house, the girls started to complain about someone knocking on their door. This happened several times and always in the same manner. They would be playing inside their room when they heard knocking on their closed door. When they went to investigate, there would be no one standing outside.

In May, my wife's niece and her boyfriend came to visit from the Netherlands. On the evening of May 8, at approximately 10:00 p.m., we all were downstairs in the family room when we heard a loud crash coming from upstairs. The noise had a distinct metallic sound. The only thing I knew of that could have produced this type of sound was a saddle rack in Sarah's room. I immediately went upstairs to investigate. The saddle rack appeared undisturbed and everything else was in place. I then checked every room upstairs without finding the source of the noise.

The next morning, we drove our guests to the airport shuttle terminal a few miles from our house. When we returned home, Monika went to the store with the girls, leaving me alone. I felt tired, so I stretched out on the love seat in the family room. I had been lying on the love seat for less than five minutes with my eyes closed when I heard the sound of squealing hinges. My eyes flew open, and I looked toward the door that led to the laundry room. As I watched, I saw the door move several inches without assistance. When I later told my mother about the incident, she suggested that Mary Bell had followed us to the new home and would probably stay with us forever.

I launched an investigation to try to confirm her suspicion. First, I used the dowsing rods and made contact with Mary Bell in the new house. To confirm that the spirit was Mary Bell, I asked her a series of questions regarding her family. Once again, she correctly answered each question, even when I tried to trick her. Second, I started to take photographs downstairs in the kitchen and living room before going to bed to see if anything would appear. I did this for several nights in a row, and on each night, captured orbs in the pictures. I decided to question Mary Bell if she had followed us from the other house and if she intended to stay with us for the rest of our lives. To no one's surprise, her answer was yes.

EPILOGUE

My life and the lives of everyone in my family changed after we became aware of a spirit living in our house. I no longer feared death because I knew that life did not end when we took our final breath, and I found comfort in the thought that one day my family would reunite. I also found comfort in the idea that I could watch over my living children after my rebirth in the spirit world. From a religious perspective, I found renewed faith with the knowledge that God's promise of eternal life was true.

I had learned a lot about ghosts during my investigation, both from observation and communication with Mary Bell, but many questions remained. The subject of ghosts has exploded onto the public's consciousness in recent years. I decided to close this book by reviewing some of the information I obtained during my research.

Are ghosts the disembodied spirits of human beings who have died?

Based on the video and photographic evidence I collected, I believe that ghosts are indeed the spirits of deceased humans. Some of the images I captured appeared to be in the form of the human body. If these images do not represent the spirit of the dead, what are they? In addition, the spirit in our house exhibited intelligence. When I contacted Mary Bell telepathically and asked if she would let us see her, she immediately began pulling energy from my video camera and soon appeared in human form. A couple months later, after Monika and Michelle called upon Mary Bell to let us see her again in human form, I captured her image in a photograph that same night in the office. A few weeks later, after I requested Mary Bell to let us see her in human form, she materialized in front of Sarah within an hour. During one session, I urged Mary Bell to communicate with us by knocking. Soon after, she started to knock on doors and on my headboard. On several occasions, I asked Mary Bell to appear in photographs or on video, and she did.

Despite growing evidence that supports an afterlife, there remains a stigma attached to the belief in ghosts. This is the result of a two-pronged attack from scientists and the Christian church. The early church sanctioned the possibility of ghosts, but wanted to restrict the occurrence of supernatural events, and attacked anyone who believed in or wanted to study ghosts. During the Spiritualist movement of the nineteenth century, the majority of mainstream church leaders loathed the movement and proclaimed it a nemesis of the pulpit. They found nothing of a biblical God or the teaching of Jesus Christ in the tales from the other side and believed that the Spiritualists drew people away from traditional teachings. Individuals who believed in the existence of spirits came under attack from both the scientific and religious. communities. The majority of scientists denounce anything associated with a supreme being. In addition to attacks from the scientific community and the church, psychologists ridiculed people who believed in ghosts and the afterlife. According to author Colin Davis, "At the beginning of the twentieth century, a new framework for understanding the return of the dead was provided by Freudian psychoanalysis. Freud exhibits a clear ambivalence towards the return of the dead. He enjoys a good ghost story as much: at the same time he equates the belief in the survival of the dead with 'savage' thinking, quite properly eradicated from the educated, civilized mind even if it continues to reside in the unconscious."

Many people who experience ghost encounters are afraid to tell anyone—and why should they when scientists tell them they are hallucinating, the Church says they are sinning by having contact with the dead, and psychologists believe their thinking is "savage." Personally, I am not afraid to tell anyone about our encounters with a ghost.

Are orbs paranormal in nature?
This question has produced intense debate among paranormal investigators. Some believe that orbs represent spirits of the deceased, while others feel they represent nothing more than dust, moisture, bugs, or reflections off bright surfaces. My opinion is that most orbs captured in photographs and on video are not paranormal, but my investigation has clearly demonstrated that some orbs have a connection with spirits. Whether they represent actual spirits or some kind of energy produced by spirits is still debatable. The first clue that pointed to our house being haunted was orbs in photographs, followed by orbs moving on video. Prior to August 2007, orbs did not appear in photos we took inside the house. Starting in August 2007, they regularly appeared in both photographs taken with digital and 35mm cameras, and on video. Orbs showed up at night and during the day. They even appeared after I covered every reflective surface downstairs.

Perhaps most significantly, I was able to introduce stimuli that influenced the orb activity. When I started to play religious music prior to our communications, the level of orbs increased dramatically. Another factor that makes me believe the orbs are paranormal is the fact that the level of activity had a direct correlation the presence of my family members. The orbs followed us from downstairs when we retired to bed. In the video where Mary Bell knocked on my headboard, an orb flies past me toward the headboard right before the knocking occurs. I contacted Mary Bell telepathically on numerous occasions and requested her to appear in photographs and each time, an orb showed up. If dust, bugs, moisture, or light reflection produced all orbs, why did I see one with my eyes in the kitchen with all the lights on? When I inquired if she traveled in the form of a small ball of light, Mary Bell answered yes. It is widely known by paranormal investigators that orbs appear in places known to be haunted, such as houses, hotels, cemeteries, etc.

Skeptics claim that orbs caught on film are nothing more than dust particles moving near the camera lens. In December 2007, we recorded an unusually high level of orbs on several consecutive nights in the master bedroom. Each time, I started the video camera prior to going into the bathroom, and it ran for approximately five minutes before I returned to bed. During this time, there was no recorded activity on the tape, however, as soon as I climbed under the sheets, the orbs started to fly. What caused this? Had dust from my body or the bed moved in front of the video camera lens? To test this, I conducted an experiment. I set up the video camera in the same position on the nightstand and turned off the lights. I then climbed into bed. After lying on the bed for several seconds, I got up and rubbed my arms vigorously to produce dust. Next, I held my pillow close to the camera and beat it for a minute, followed by holding the comforter in the same position and shaking it for thirty seconds. This activity should have produced dust close to the camera lens, but no orbs appeared on this video.

Why do ghosts appear as orbs?
I believe ghosts take the form of orbs because it allows them to move easier within their realm. In her book, *Ghost Worlds: A Guide to Poltergeists, Portals, Ecto-mist & Spirit Behavior,* researcher Melba Goodwyn suggests that energy is behind the ghost's orb appearance. "Orbs require less energy than full-bodied ghosts, enabling them to exist more easily in our dimensional frequency. At times they are able to appear denser or larger and they can manifest as a partial or full apparition." Mary Bell Wilson fits this definition of a spirit orb. "They seem to exhibit personalities and respond to telepathy; they are very telepathic by nature, and welcome communication in this way. They interact with people on a personal, emotional level and are capable of expressing feelings."

Why are ghosts more active at night?
There are numerous theories that try to explain why ghosts seem to appear more at night than during the day. During my communications with Mary Bell, I believe

she gave me the answer. Many people accept that while we sleep, our spirits travel outside the body. According to Mary Bell, she has visited my spirit and the spirits of my family while we slept, and these visits occurred every night. If this is true, it makes sense that ghosts would be more active when they can interact easily with the living.

Do ghosts absorb energy in order to manifest?
Ghost researchers have reported this phenomenon for many years, and based on evidence gathered during my investigation, this is true. In the days leading up to Mary Bell's manifestation on September 10, she pulled energy from the batteries of my video camera. This occurred over several consecutive nights. Each time, the image on the screen shook and the camera made a grinding noise. On the night of September 10, this occurred four times. Prior to Mary Bell appearing to Monika and Sarah in late October and December, we experienced the same grinding noise on clock radios, the television, and computer speakers. Some researchers suggest that spirits need a lot of energy to manifest due to the density of our atmosphere.

How do ghosts communicate with the living?
Our first efforts to communicate with the spirit of Mary Bell Wilson involved asking questions and waiting for a verbal response. We recorded our first breakthrough when I used telepathy. For several days prior to September 10,

I called upon Mary Bell telepathically to appear in human form. She immediately started to absorb energy from my video camera, and I was able to capture her image in a photograph and on video. In October, I implored Mary Bell to communicate by knocking. Within days, she started to knock on doors. During the week before my visit at the Fort Collins Museum, Mary Bell began communicating with me while I slept. This continued until January 2008. In December, she threw pictures off the wall on consecutive nights to get our attention. One afternoon, she caused a music box to move and start playing. Another time, she lifted the telephone by my bed off its cradle. Starting in late November, we began communicating with Mary Bell via the dowsing rods.

Do ghosts retain intelligence?

The spirit of Mary Bell Wilson has often demonstrated the ability to reason. She responded to musical stimuli. She displayed a social personality when she followed us upstairs at night. Mary Bell answered my request to appear before us and gained our attention by knocking and rapping. Whenever I communicated with Mary Bell using the dowsing rods, she always correctly answered my questions about both her family and mine. Besides intelligence, I believe spirits retain their personalities. According to family histories, Mary Bell was a loving mother and good Christian woman. She seemed to watch over our children and responded when we played Christian hymns prior to communicating with her.

Can ghosts be captured on film?

People have been taking ghost photographs for at least a hundred years. Some of these images are famous, including the SS Watertown ghosts and The Brown Lady of Raynham Hall. Starting in the late 1980s, orbs began appearing in numerous pictures. Because orbs showed up with such regularity, some paranormal investigators questioned their validity as supernatural entities. During my investigation, I used three different types of cameras to record spirit activity: a Sony digital camera with a nightshot feature, a Kodak disposable 35mm camera, and a Sony video camera with nightshot capability. I was never able to capture orbs with my digital camera set on nightshot. The video camera recorded both orbs and Mary Bell manifested in human form while set on nightshot. I retained all of the original videos that contain evidence as well as the digital camera memory stick with the pictures of Mary Bell in human form. I am willing to allow experts examine them to confirm they are authentic.

Do ghosts have psychic ability?

Many parapsychologists and psychics believe all people are born with varying degrees of psychic ability. According to psychic Michele Anderson, this psychic ability is available to all because it is an attribute of the soul. Perhaps when a person dies, their psychic abilities are unlocked. When I first started to communicate with Mary Bell using the dowsing rods, I was surprised to learn she knew intimate details about my life and family. She correctly identified my relatives by name and even knew where some of them were born or buried. She knew the name of my ex-wife and the names of family pets that had died. Some researchers feel that when we die our spirits can see things more clearly and the mind opens to possibilities previously unknown to us.

Can a living person tell when a ghost is close by?
People have reported various signs warning them of a spirit's presence such as feeling cold, hearing noises, observing shadows, etc. During my investigation, I personally experienced some of these. There were times when the temperature suddenly dropped around me for no apparent reason. One night as I tucked the kids in bed, I felt a cold spot over my right shoulder. When Monika spotted the shadow person and later Mary Bell's spirit manifested upstairs, goosebumps covered her arms, which according to paranormal author Melba Goodwyn, "should never be discounted, because they are definitely associated with a ghostly presence."

In the master bedroom, I often had the sensation of someone touching my exposed feet as I lay on the bed or feeling pressure on the lower part of my legs. Sarah also experienced the sensation of someone sitting on the end of her bed and then getting off the mattress. On the night Mary Bell knocked on my headboard, I had no idea she was so close until I heard the knocking and then felt her climb onto the bed and move toward me. There were times I saw strange lights moving around the room. One night as I talked on the phone with my brother, I saw shimmering light moving around the family room. Monika, Sarah, and I have all heard unexplained voices. The behavior of our dog Rosie was another indicator of Mary Bell's presence. At times, Rosie would be asleep on the couch and then take off running out of the room for no apparent reason. One night Rosie cowered at the top of the stairs. She would not move across the landing even with Sarah squatting in the open door of her bedroom and imploring her to come. Sarah finally had to pick up Rosie and carry her into her room. On numerous occasions, Rosie would stare toward a spot for no apparent reason for several minutes before moving on.

Do ghosts remain with their families?

For the majority of people the most important thing in their life is the love of their family. Thus, when we imagine the afterlife, we like to think of spending eternity with those we love. Once I had established that Mary Bell Wilson's spirit lived with us, I wondered if the spirits of her family members lived with her. If an orb represents a single spirit, we definitely had more than one spirit in our house. I have filmed as many as eight orbs moving at the same time with the video camera. In addition, the photograph that I took in the office appears to show a spirit that is not Mary Bell. When I asked Mary Bell if she was with her family in the spirit world, the answer was yes. She responded the same way when I questioned her if she visited with them every day. Mary Bell also answered yes when I inquired if she met family members when they crossed over into the spirit world.

Do spirits socialize with other spirits?

Does the spirit world function like the physical world? Do spirits meet and fall in love with other spirits? According to Mary Bell, they do. Her answers suggest that spirits not only socialize with other spirits, but with the living as well. Mary Bell responded positively when questioned if spirits attended movies in theaters with other spirits and the living. She also said that spirits continue to worship God, which might indicate that spirits live in a collective society. Mary Bell's husband Charles Wilson, remarried soon after her death, and when I asked her if she was still married in the spirit world, her answer was no. Mary Bell also told me that spirits could fall in love with the living. Author J. Allan Danelek advised in an email that Mary Bell might develop a relationship with me: "If you are actually in contact with the spirit of this young woman, don't be surprised if she actually becomes infatuated with you personally, and perhaps even grows jealous if you don't continue to respond to her. Remember, you are dealing with the intact personality of a very young girl here, so you need to speak to her in that context." I personally believe that Mary Bell's interest in me stemmed from the fact that I was the one communicating with her. Other than the two incidents in which she tossed pictures off the wall, Mary Bell did not exhibit jealous behavior when we did not respond to her.

Is the spirit world close to ours?

I believe that the spirit world is in such close proximity to ours that they can move easily between both worlds. According to Mary Bell's answers, spirits travel around the world, seek out entertainment, socialize, worship, fall in love, etc. She told me that she had traveled by car, but not airplane. What does this mean? Why would she need to travel by car? The fact she knows about cars and movie theaters indicates Mary Bell is aware of technological advances since her death in 1886.

Brigham Young had this to say regarding the spirit world: "Where is the spirit world? It is right here. Do the good and evil spirits go together? Yes they do...do they go beyond the boundaries of the organized earth? No, they do not...can you see it with your natural eyes?

No. Can you see spirits in this room? No. Suppose the Lord should touch your eyes that you might see, could you, then see the spirits? Yes, as plainly as you now see the bodies." Young goes on to describe life in the spirit world: "The postmortal spirit world is an actual place where spirits reside and where they converse together the same as we do on the earth. Life and work and activity all continue in the spirit world. Men have the same talents and intelligence there, which they had in this life. They possess the same attitudes, inclinations, and feelings there which they had in this life."

The Reverend Simeon Stefanidakis of the First Spiritual Temple agrees that the spirit world is nearby. "The spirit world is right here, where we are. We do not have to travel in order to get to the spirit world. It is not separated from the Earth plane by distance, as we perceive distance. What separates the Earth plane from the spirit world is dimension."

Do spirits watch over the living?
If spirits retain their intelligence and memory, it only makes sense they would want to stay in contact with people they left behind. There have been so many sightings of ghosts by grieving relatives that paranormal investigators have given this kind of spirit a classification of their own: Familial Personalities. My late grandmother reported seeing the ghost of her second husband shortly

after he died. It is clear in our case that Mary Bell stayed near her family's farm in order to be close to her relatives, especially her daughter, Leona. I believe when a person dies they retain the ability to watch over their living family members. I do not think a spirit watches over the living around the clock, but they can view them whenever they feel the need.

Do spirits react to what the living do?
Since spirits watch the living as they go about their daily routines, it makes sense they would react to the actions of living persons. Mary Bell responded to various stimuli I introduced, as well as telepathic communication and communication via the dowsing rods. Mary Bell was more active when I paid attention to her. J. Allan Danelek suggested that Mary Bell might go away if we stopped paying attention to her. Now that it appears she has followed us to our new home, I do not believe she is going anywhere anytime soon.

Can the living bring spirits into their lives?
When I started to investigate our house for spirit activity, I did not expect to find any spirits living with us, even though we had subtle clues that a spirit might be present. Of course, at that time, I did not know the history of the land where our house sat or that the former owners of the land had a daughter named Mary Bell who died at a

young age, or we might have a gravesite in our backyard. Because Mary Bell was already present when I started my investigation, I immediately began to collect evidence that confirmed her existence. I have often wondered if it would be possible to bring a spirit into your home if that spirit had no obvious reason for being there. I believe that many spirits move freely throughout their realm and these spirits might respond to contact by living persons. To do this, I recommend doing activity that lets the spirit know your intentions. This may involve taking random photographs, shooting video in both normal and low-light conditions, attempting to communicate through a séance, or by using telepathy. At some point, introducing stimuli such as religious music may influence the results.

Some people think that by welcoming spirits into your home, you may allow evil spirits or demons into your life. I have never experienced anything like this, but that does not mean it is not true. My advice is to use caution. After making contact with a spirit, if you have any reason to be afraid or believe the spirit's presence is negative, you should stop trying to communicate. If you are nervous about welcoming an unknown spirit into your life, but remain curious, you could always try to contact a relative who has died. In my opinion, if more people contacted spirits and documented their experience with photographs and video, we would see a rise in ghost sightings. I also believe that many people would be surprised to discover they have a spirit living with them, even if there is not obvious history that supports their presence.

Is it dangerous to communicate with spirits?
If a person contacted a priest and asked them this question, they would undoubtedly say yes. Most religions teach that we are to maintain a division between the world of the living and that of spirits. I personally do not understand this way of thinking. Many people find comfort in contacting deceased loved ones. Provided it does not become an obsession, what is wrong with this? The one worry I have in regards to contacting spirits is making a connection with an angry spirit. Since spirits retain their personalities, I do not think I would welcome the spirit of a murderer or cruel person into my life. Ghost hunters around the world have reported being pushed, pinched, and hit by unseen assailants. Mary Bell is a passive spirit, yet this did not stop her from throwing pictures off the wall. If someone had been standing nearby when Mary Bell did this, that person would have been injured.

Does a spirit become a ghost when they fail to cross over to the proper realm?
It is a widely held belief that spirits become ghosts because they do not cross over to the proper realm at the time of their death. There are many theories on why this happens including, the spirit had unfinished business on

earth, they did not realize they had died, or died young and was not ready to go. One of the reasons some paranormal investigators believe this is because ghosts tend to stay in a location for a certain amount of time and then vanish. I asked Mary Bell more than once if she knew that she was dead, and every time the answer was yes. I also inquired numerous times if she was in the place she was supposed to be, and again the answer came back as yes. If she is in the proper realm, why did Mary Bell reach out to us? My guess is that she stayed close to our house because her original burial site was nearby. In addition, she appears to be attracted to our children. It is also possible that other members of the Webster family have been inside our house, which could explain the large number of orbs captured on video, and the image in the photograph taken in the office.

What is the spirit world like?

Until someone invents a method that allows us to enter the spirit world without first dying, or lets us have indisputable communication with spirits, we will never know what awaits us when we die. Early spiritualists agreed that all planets have spirit worlds or spheres. The first sphere, which is closet to Earth, was imperfect with little light. The land was barren without flowers or trees. Some spirits in this sphere had houses, but they were poorly constructed. In this sphere disorder reigns.

The landscapes and all aspects varied in each sphere becoming more beautiful as one progressed higher. The spiritualists believed that people who were sinful and evil in body arrived the same way in the spirit world where they gravitated to others with similar natures. These earthbound spirits having retained their earthly passions and propensities, found it difficult to build up their spirit bodies.

Rev. Stefanidakis of the First Spiritual Temple offers this opinion on what happens to a spirit. "As time passes on, we integrate more and more of our recent earth life and its experiences into the essence of the spirit. More and more of our family and loved ones join us. And eventually, we move further along the spirit world, into areas which are more separated, in terms of vibration, from the earth plane. We can always draw back, closer to the earthly condition, in order to communicate with earthly loved ones or family members. So, we are never separated from our beloved, no matter where they or we may be."

According to Rev. Stefanidakis, the astral plane is closely linked to the earth plane and within the astral plane, there exists an exact replica of the earth plane, with houses, cities, mountains, people, etc. He also suggests that even while on the earth plane, we are spirit, and have a connection to the spirit world.

I agree that the spirit realm is close to the realm occupied by the living. I also agree that the spirit realm closely resembles the earth plane, but whether this is because they experience a replica of earth, or continue to share our earthly plane but in a higher frequency is unknown.

Is there a Heaven and Hell?

Humanity has pondered the possibility of Heaven and Hell for thousands of years, and I wish I could say that I have a definitive answer, but I do not. When I questioned Mary Bell, she told me that both Heaven and Hell existed. What does this mean? Are they states of consciousness or actual physical places? I personally do not believe in Hell as a place where sinners go to burn for eternity. I believe, as did Brigham Young, that God is a forgiving God and would rather rehabilitate than punish. Perhaps the spirits of sinners remain separated from other spirits until they are able to function properly. Mary Bell did say that she has seen both God and Jesus, indicating a divine presence in the spirit world. There is enough evil in the world today to suggest that Satan is real and busy at work corrupting the minds of men. Let us hope that if this is the case his influence does not carry over into the spirit world. Mary Bell said that spirits could not hurt other spirits and there were no wars in the spirit realm, signs that evil does not exist where she resides.

Can spirits time travel?

I was surprised when Mary Bell told me she had the ability to travel through time, and has traveled back to a time before her birth, and as far as five hundred years into the future. Many scientists believe people will eventually be able to travel through time. I had always assumed that spirits would not track the passing of time; however, Mary Bell indicated this was not true. If spirits can freely move through what we know as time, the question becomes, why would they do this? As a history buff, I would appreciate the opportunity to travel back in time and witness historical events. Do spirits travel through time for amusement? Perhaps their time travel is part of an ongoing education in which they review events from their past lives. Why and how spirits move through time are questions that we may never be able to answer.

Do spirits live forever?

According to Mary Bell, spirits do not age, nor do they die—and why should they when it is generally accepted that spirits are comprised of energy? I can accept that spirits live forever, but I do wonder what is to become of spirits if they remain closely attached to the earth plane. The earth will not exist forever. At some point, the sun will turn supernova and destroy the earth. Perhaps the earth will survive its physical death in much the same way as a spirit—as energy. NASA studies of the earth's water and energy cycles have found that solar energy drives the water cycle, and the interaction of water with radiation modulates these energy exchanges—energy is transferred, not lost. Russian experiments performed aboard space stations have discovered significant electron and positron fluxes with energies of more than decades of megaelectron volts (MeV) in the Earth's radiation belts. Their research has shown that in outer space near the earth exists some efficient mechanism capable of accelerating electrons to energies of more than decades of MeV. No force in the physical world has the ability to destroy energy.

Final thoughts

When it comes to investigating the paranormal and ghosts, we simply do not possess the technology to prove that life after death is a normal part of the human experience. I personally believe that the barrier between the spirit realm and the realm of the living is thinning to the point we will one day be able to communicate with spirits on a daily basis, but until that day arrives, we must be content to interact with spirits using the technology we have available. It is my hope that others who are investigating the phenomenon of ghosts will uncover evidence that conclusively proves their existence. Until that happens, I will be content in the knowledge that our experience with Mary Bell has further opened the door into understanding ghosts and their place in our world.

APPENDIX

*H*aving communicated with the spirit of Mary Bell Wilson for almost five months, I was continually amazed at the intimate details she knew about my family. Despite my attempts to trick her by using false information in the questions, she always knew the correct answer. How was this possible? Does Mary Bell possess superconscious telepathy, which allows her to tap into the superconscious to access the collective wisdom of the human species? Do our minds open up to all knowledge after we die, thus, whenever I posed a question to Mary Bell, all she had to do was think about it and the answer came to her automatically? If this was true, then Mary Bell should be able to answer other questions. How would she respond if I inquired about some of the famous mysteries from science and history? If I asked her to identify Jack the Ripper or confirm if an alien spacecraft crash-landed in Roswell, New Mexico, would she answer? Of course, there is no way to confirm if her responses were true, but I thought it might be fun. Here are the results.

QUESTION: If Lee Harvey Oswald was the only person who shot President Kennedy, cross the rods.

ANSWER: Yes.

COMMENT: Oswald had the means and motive, but did he act alone? I have always believed that a lone gunman willing to sacrifice his own life would be harder to stop than a conspiracy of individuals.

QUESTION: If the Mafia was involved in plotting the assassination of President John Kennedy, uncross the rods.

ANSWER: No.

COMMENT: Why would the Mafia have risked the negative exposure from being involved in the assassination? If they wanted to go after Kennedy, all they had to do was leak information regarding his personal life. It is widely believed that J. Edgar Hoover did not go after organized crime because they blackmailed him with his homosexuality.

QUESTION: If Fidel Castro was involved in plotting the assassination of President John Kennedy, uncross the rods.

ANSWER: No.

COMMENT: Castro had a motive, but it was not in the best interest of his government to do so. If he were linked to the assassination of President Kennedy, it would have given the United States more incentive to get rid of him.

QUESTION: If the Central Intelligence Agency was involved in plotting the assassination of President John Kennedy, uncross the rods.

ANSWER: No.

COMMENT: This answer did not surprise me. If the press had discovered that the CIA was involved in the assassination of an American president, it would have killed the agency as we know it.

QUESTION: If Cuban exiles were involved in plotting the assassination of President John Kennedy, uncross the rods.

ANSWER: Yes.

COMMENT: Evidence gathered by the House Select Committee on Assassinations implicated certain violent Cuban exiles in President Kennedy's murder. These exiles had worked jointly with CIA operatives in violent acts against Castro's Cuba. Why would Cuban exiles work with Oswald in a plot to kill Kennedy? Perhaps their mutual disdain for Kennedy united them. Perhaps the exiles wanted Kennedy dead but couldn't find anyone crazy enough until Oswald came along.

QUESTION: If Lyndon Baines Johnson was involved in plotting the assassination of President John Kennedy, cross the rods.

ANSWER: No.

COMMENT: Numerous conspiracy theories accuse then Vice President Johnson of being behind the assassination of President Kennedy. These theories range from Johnson wanting to kill Kennedy because he feared that Kennedy would replace him on the upcoming presidential ticket, to Johnson conspiring with military contractors who feared that Kennedy would soon end American involvement in the Vietnam War. Lyndon Johnson may have been ambitious and felt some animosity toward President Kennedy, but there has never been solid evidence to connect him to the assassination.

QUESTION: If Lucien Sarti was involved in the assassination of President Kennedy, cross the rods.

ANSWER: No.

COMMENT: In an article published by *Rolling Stone* magazine, Lucien Sarti claimed to have shot at Kennedy from the grassy knoll. I expanded upon the previous question by using the name of a would-be gunman. As expected, the answer was no.

QUESTION: If Mac Wallace was involved in the assassination of President Kennedy, cross the rods.

ANSWER: No.

COMMENT: Lyndon Johnson was associated professionally and personally to a convicted murderer, Malcolm "Mac" Wallace, who supposedly has been linked to the Kennedy assassination through testimony and forensic evidence.

QUESTION: If the Soviet Union was involved in plotting the assassination of President Kennedy, cross the rods.

ANSWER: No.

COMMENT: A suggested motive for the KGB's involvement was revenge for the humiliation of the Cuban Missile Crisis. Personally, I see no benefit to the Russians from killing Kennedy. Fidel

Castro was not going anywhere and the United States was escalating its involvement in Vietnam. Furthermore, while the Soviets may have felt a sense of public embarrassment by the outcome of the missile crisis, in truth, they had to feel somewhat vindicated by the final results, after all, the United States did remove its own missiles from Turkey, and more importantly, the Soviets secured Kennedy's promise to not invade Cuba.

QUESTION: If Israel was involved in plotting the assassination of President John Kennedy, cross the rods.

ANSWER: No.

COMMENT: According to this theory, the Israeli government was displeased with Kennedy for his stand against their pursuit of a top-secret nuclear program at the Negev Nuclear Research Center or they were angry over his sympathies with Arabs and his use of former Nazis in the American space program. When you consider that Israel was still a young, struggling country at the time, which depended heavily on American financial and military support, it makes no sense that they would risk alienating the United States by getting involved in the assassination of an American president.

QUESTION: If Amelia Earhart was spying for the United States at the time of her disappearance, cross the rods.

ANSWER: No.

COMMENT: On June 1, 1937, famous aviator Amelia Earhart took off with her navigator Fred Noonan from Miami and started what was supposed to be a flight around the world. They disappeared on July 2, 1937, over the Pacific Ocean. Almost immediately, rumors started that Amelia Earhart had been on a secret mission to spy on the Japanese on behalf of the American government. By 1949, both the United Press and U.S. Army intelligence had concluded these rumors were groundless. Jackie Cochran (a pioneer aviator and friend of Earhart) made a postwar search of numerous files in Japan and was convinced the Japanese were not involved in Earhart's disappearance.

QUESTION: If Amelia Earhart was captured by the Japanese, cross the rods.

ANSWER: No.

COMMENT: Several books propose that Japanese soldiers captured Earhart and Noonan who they later executed. No independent confirmation or support has ever emerged for any of these claims.

The most likely scenario is that Earhart's plane went down in the Pacific Ocean taking Earhart and Noonan with it.

QUESTION: If UFOs are causing airplanes and ships to disappear in the Bermuda Triangle, cross the rods.

ANSWER: Yes.

COMMENT: The legendary Bermuda Triangle, or Devil's Triangle, runs from Bermuda to Puerto Rico to Miami and back to Bermuda. A number of aircraft and ships have mysteriously disappeared in the area. One theory regarding these disappearances involves alien abduction. Some suggest the Bermuda Triangle is one of two portals used by "human-like" aliens, to travel from their planet to ours. According to this theory, the Bermuda Triangle is not actually a triangle, but is constantly in motion and intensity. The disappearances occur when the craft gets caught in the center or within the first two outward radiating rings. The occurrence takes place twenty-five times a year and lasts twenty-eight minutes. The aliens' technology enables them to use time compression, solar power, and the ability to reduce friction for traveling across vast distances.

QUESTION: If there is a real Bigfoot in the Pacific Northwest, uncross the rods.

ANSWER: No.

COMMENT: Of all the legendary monsters, this one, I thought, might trigger a positive response. The Pacific Northwest has huge tracts of undeveloped land covered in dense forest—a perfect hiding place with plenty of food for a creature to survive. However, people have trekked into the forest for years with sophisticated equipment in an effort to collect evidence of Bigfoot without success.

QUESTION: If there is a real Loch Ness monster, uncross the rods.

ANSWER: No.

COMMENT: An unknown creature that resembles an extinct Plesiosaur allegedly lives in Scotland's Loch Ness. Evidence of the creature's existence is largely anecdotal. Skeptics dispute the collected photographic material. There has not been any other physical evidence including skeletal remains, capture of a live animal, definitive tissue samples, or spoor uncovered. Because of the lack of evidence in this case, Mary Bell's answer did not surprise me.

QUESTION: If space aliens made the first crop circles, uncross the rods.

ANSWER: No.

COMMENT: No one knows when the first crop circles appeared; however, in 1991 two men from Southampton, England, claimed to have conceived the idea as a prank. Doug Bower and Dave Chorley made their crop circles using planks, rope, and wire. They used a four-foot-long plank attached to a rope to create circles eight feet in diameter. Despite their confession, many people do not believe the circles are man-made. British astronomer Gerald Hawkins argues that some of the circles display a level of complexity that would be difficult to recreate on paper, let alone in a field after dark.

QUESTION: If the ancient Egyptians and Mayans received aide from space aliens, uncross the rods.

ANSWER: No.

COMMENT: Evidence for ancient astronauts is said to include the existence of ancient monuments and megalithic ruins such as the Giza pyramids of Egypt, Machu Picchu in Peru, or Baalbek in Lebanon. Supporters contend that people could not have built these structures with the technical abilities and tools of the time and further argue that many could not be duplicated even today.

QUESTION: If space aliens helped in the design and construction of the Nazca Lines, uncross the rods.

ANSWER: Yes.

COMMENT: The Nazca Lines are located in the Nazca Desert. They are a series of geoglyphs on the floor of the desert, a high arid plateau that stretches 53 miles between the towns of Nazca and Palpa on the Pampas de Jumana in Peru. The Nazca culture is thought to have created the lines between 200 BCE and AD 700. There are hundreds of individual figures with a wide rage of complexity, created by removing the iron oxide–coated pebbles that cover the surface of the Nasca Desert. Once the gravel has been removed, the lines contrast sharply with the surroundings because of the light-colored earth underneath. UFO theories contend that extraterrestrials helped create the lines because they can only be observed from high altitude. Mary Bell's answer puzzled me. Previously, she stated that there were no people or creatures alive on other planets. Additionally, her answers to the questions regarding crop circles, and the ancient Egyptians and Mayans, indicates that space aliens are not real. Why then did she give a positive response to this question?

QUESTION: If the civilization of Atlantis was real, cross the rods.

ANSWER: Yes.

COMMENT: The lost continent of Atlantis is a legendary island first mentioned in Plato's dialogues *Timaeus* and *Critias*. Plato claimed that Atlantis was located "beyond the Pillars of Heracles," and was a naval power that conquered many parts of Western Europe and Africa 9,000 years before the time of Solon, or approximately 9500 BCE. He wrote that Atlantis sank into the ocean on a single day and night of misfortune after a failed attempt to invade Athens. Researchers have attempted to locate Atlantis for many years. Several locations have been suggested for the location of Atlantis, with most of the historically proposed locations in or near the Mediterranean Sea.

QUESTION: If Noah's Ark is on Mount Ararat, uncross the rods.

ANSWER: No.

COMMENT: According to Abrahamic religions, Noah's Ark was a large vessel built at God's command to save Noah, his family, and the core stock of the world's animals from the Great Flood. The story is told in chapters 6-9 of the book of Genesis, with later variations in the Qur'an and a number of other sources. According to Genesis 8:4 the Ark came to rest "in the mountains of Ararat," though in the Qur'an the landing place is said to be Al-Judi. Two main candidates have emerged for exploration, the so-called Ararat anomaly near the main summit of Ararat, and the separate site at Duripinar near Dogubayazit, 18 miles south of the Greater Ararat summit.

QUESTION: If Noah's Ark is real, uncross the rods.

ANSWER: Yes.

COMMENT: I elected to follow up my previous question regarding Noah's Ark since it neither confirmed nor dismissed the existence of the Ark.

QUESTION: If the Ark of the Covenant is located in Ethiopia, cross the rods.

ANSWER: Yes.

COMMENT: The Ethiopian Orthodox Church in Axum, Ethiopia is the only one in the world that claims to possess the Ark of the Covenant. They keep it under constant guard in a "treasury" near the Church of Our Lady Mary of Zion.

QUESTION: If it is possible for a person to levitate, uncross the rods.

ANSWER: No.

COMMENT: Can objects, people, and animals lift into the air without visible physical means and float or fly? According to those who practice levitation the answer is yes. Levitation is a phenomenon of psychokinesis reported to have occurred in mediumship, shamanism, trances, mystical rapture, and demonic possession. In some cases, the levitation is spontaneous, while spiritual or magical adepts are said to be able to control it consciously. Levitation occurs through two methods: actual levitation, and creating the illusion of levitation using clever mechanics, lighting arrangements, and other means.

QUESTION: If it is possible for a person to teleport, uncross the rods.

ANSWER: No.

COMMENT: Teleportation is the movement of objects from one place to another, more or less instantaneously, without traveling through space. One proposed means of teleportation is the transmission of data to reconstruct an object or organism at its destination. The use of this form of teleportation as a means of transport for humans still has considerable unresolved technical and philosophical issues. How to record the human body, particularly the brain, with sufficient accuracy and be able to reconstruct it, and whether destroying a human in one place and recreating a copy elsewhere would provide a sufficient experience of continuity of existence.

QUESTION: If spirits are reincarnated, uncross the rods.

ANSWER: No.

COMMENT: I had asked this question before, but I thought that I had phrased it poorly, so I wanted to try again. The answer remained the same.

QUESTION: If the Shroud of Turin is the actual burial cloth of Jesus Christ, uncross the rods.

ANSWER: No.

COMMENT: Controversy surrounds the Shroud of Turin, a linen cloth bearing the image of a man who has been physically traumatized in a manner consistent with crucifixion and believed by many to have been worn by Jesus Christ at the time of his burial. There is intense debate among scientists, people of faith, historians, and writers regarding where, when, and how the shroud and its images were created. Radiocarbon dating in 1988 by three independent teams of scientists indicated that the shroud was made during the Middle Ages, about 1,300 years after Jesus lived. Believers of the Shroud immediately claimed bias and error in the tests.

QUESTION: If vampires are real, uncross the rods.

ANSWER: No.

COMMENT: Vampires are a fixture of popular culture in film and books. They are mythological or folkloric revenants, who subsist by feeding on the blood of the living. Vampire legends began in Eastern Europe and spread into Western European culture through folkloric tales that told of undead vampires who visited loved ones and caused mischief or deaths in places they inhabited while alive.

QUESTION: If an asteroid striking the earth killed off the dinosaurs, uncross the rods.

ANSWER: Yes.

COMMENT: Dinosaurs were the dominant vertebrate animals of terrestrial ecosystems from the late Triassic period to the end of the Cretaceous period. Walter Alvarez and colleagues brought the asteroid collision theory to wide attention in 1980. This theory links the extinction event at the end of the Cretaceous period to a bolide impact approximately 65.5 million years ago. The bulk of the evidence now suggests that a 5 to 15 kilometer wide bolide hit in the vicinity of the Yucatan Peninsula, creating the 170 kilometer wide Chicxulub Crater and triggering the mass extinction.

QUESTION: If spontaneous human combustion is real, cross the rods.

ANSWER: Yes.

COMMENT: Spontaneous human combustion refers to the belief that the human body sometimes burns without an external source of ignition. There is much speculation and controversy regarding SHC, for it is not a proven natural phenomenon. Many theories and hypotheses have attempted to explain how SHC could occur, but those, which rely on current scientific understanding, say that instances mistaken for spontaneous combustion actually required a source of ignition.

QUESTION: If mermaids are real, uncross the rods.

ANSWER: No.

COMMENT: Mermaids are a legendary aquatic creature with the head and torso of human female and the tail of a fish. The male version of a mermaid is called a merman. There has never been scientific evidence that supports the existence of mermaids; therefore, I am not surprised by Mary Bell's answer.

QUESTION: If the Amityville Horror is a true story, uncross the rods.

ANSWER: No.

COMMENT: The Amityville Horror is perhaps America's most famous ghost story, popularized in a book by Jay Anson based on the experiences of George and Kathleen Lutz. In November of 1974, Ronald DeFeo Jr., shot and killed six members of his family inside the family's large Dutch Colonial house in Amityville, a suburban neighborhood located on the south shore of Long Island, New York. In December 1975, George and Kathleen Lutz and their children moved into the house on 112 Ocean Avenue. The family fled the house after twenty-eight days, claiming they had been terrorized by paranormal phenomena. Skeptics immediately attacked the story as a work of fiction. William Weber, the defense lawyer for Ronald DeFeo Jr., said that the entire story was a hoax created by him and the Lutzes over many bottles of wine.

QUESTION: If an alien spacecraft crashed at Roswell, New Mexico, in 1947, uncross the rods.

ANSWER: Yes.

COMMENT: The most famous UFO incident in history occurred near Roswell, New Mexico, on July 7, 1947. It has since become the subject of rumor, intense speculation, and questioning. Many UFO proponents believe that the United States Air Force recovered a crashed alien craft from a ranch near Roswell. The Air Force claims a top-secret research balloon crashed.

QUESTION: If the government recovered the bodies of aliens from the Roswell crash site, cross the rods.

ANSWER: Yes.

COMMENT: Several eyewitnesses reported that the bodies of extraterrestrials were recovered at the Roswell crash site and later given autopsies. There is no evidence to substantiate these reports.

QUESTION: If Sam Sheppard killed his wife Marilyn Sheppard, uncross the rods.

ANSWER: Yes.

COMMENT: Samuel Sheppard was an osteopathic physician convicted of killing his pregnant wife Marilyn Sheppard in the early morning hours of July 4, 1954, after a controversial murder trial. He claimed that a bushy-haired man killed his wife. The case was the inspiration of the popular television series, *The Fugitive*.

QUESTION: If Lizzie Borden killed her parents, cross the rods.

ANSWER: Yes.

COMMENT: On August 4, 1892, Andrew Borden and his wife Abby Borden were bludgeoned to death by a hatchet. Authorities arrested his daughter Lizzie Borden for the crime. She was ultimately acquitted. No one else was ever arrested or tried and she remained notorious in American folklore.

QUESTION: If Bruno Hauptmann killed the Lindbergh baby, uncross the rods.

ANSWER: No.

COMMENT: The Lindbergh baby kidnapping remains one of the most famous murder cases. It began on March 1, 1932, with the kidnapping of the infant son of famous aviator Charles Lindbergh from the family's New Jersey home. On May 12, 1932, the infant's body was discovered within a few miles of the Lindbergh estate. In 1943, a gold certificate from the ransom money turned up that had a license plate number written on it. The New York license plate belonged to a dark blue Dodge sedan owned by Bruno Richard Hauptmann, a German carpenter who had illegally immigrated to the United States. The authorities arrested Hauptmann and charged him with the murder. Evidence against Hauptmann included over $14,000 in ransom money found in his garage, a handmade ladder supposedly used in the kidnapping, and testimony alleging handwriting and spelling similarities to that found on the ransom notes. Hauptmann was positively identified as the man to whom the ransom money was delivered, and had been seen in the area around the Lindbergh estate on the day of the kidnapping. Convicted and sentenced to death, Hauptmann denied his guilt to the very end. On April 3, 1936, authorities executed Hauptmann in the electric chair at the New Jersey State Prison.

QUESTION: If Jon Benet Ramsey was killed by one of her parents, uncross the rods.

ANSWER: No.

COMMENT: Six-year-old Jon Benet Ramsey was killed on December 25, 1996, inside the house of her wealthy parents, John and Patsy Ramsey. Her body was discovered inside the wine cellar under a blanket. She died from strangulation and a skull fracture. Several theories emerged that linked her parents to the crime. One suggested that Patsy Ramsey injured her child in a fit of rage after the girl wet her bed and then proceeded to kill her in a rage or to cover up the original injury. Another claims that John Ramsey sexually abused his daughter and murdered her as a cover. In July of 2008, several months after I questioned Mary Bell Wilson about the murder, the Boulder police announced that new DNA testing failed to turn up evidence linking anyone from the Ramsey family with Jon Benet's death.

QUESTION: If Arthur Leigh Allen was the Zodiac Killer, uncross the rods.

ANSWER: Yes.

◆

COMMENT: In the late 1960s, a serial killer terrorized Northern California. The killer coined the name "Zodiac" in a series of taunting letters sent to the press. Included in the letters were four cryptograms or ciphers, three of which remained unsolved. The Zodiac murdered five known victims in Benicia, Vallejo, Lake Berryessa, and San Francisco between December 1968 and October 1969. The prime suspect in the Zodiac murders was Arthur Leigh Allen. Many believed him to have been the infamous Zodiac serial killer but authorities never charged Allen. Much of the case for Allen as the serial killer is based on a considerable amount of circumstantial evidence.

QUESTION: If O. J. Simpson killed Nichole Brown Simpson and Ron Goldman, cross the rods.

ANSWER: Yes.

COMMENT: O.J. Simpson, a former football star, was accused of killing his ex-wife Nichole Brown Simpson and her friend Ronald Goldman. Shortly before midnight on June 12, 1994, Brown and Goldman were found fatally stabbed outside Brown's Brundy Drive condominium in the

Brentwood area of Los Angeles, California. Evidence found and collected at the scene led police to suspect that O. J. Simpson was the murderer. Simpson was acquitted after a lengthy criminal trial.

QUESTION: If D. B. Cooper survived after parachuting from the airplane, uncross the rods.

ANSWER: No.

COMMENT: D. B. Cooper, aka Dan Cooper, is an alias of an aircraft hijacker who, on November 25, 1971, after receiving a ransom payout of $200,000, jumped from the back of a Boeing 727 as it flew over the Pacific Northwest. Despite hundreds of suspects through the years, no conclusive evidence has surfaced regarding Cooper's identity or whereabouts. The FBI believes that Cooper did not survive the jump.

QUESTION: If Marilyn Monroe was murdered, uncross the rods.

ANSWER: No.

COMMENT: Marilyn Monroe was a Hollywood icon whose legend has continued to grow in the decades after her sudden death at the age of 36. The LA coroners' office ruled her death as a probable suicide. Monroe was reputed to have been involved with both Robert Kennedy and John F. Kennedy at the time of her death, and some conspiracy theorists believe that the Kennedys had Monroe killed to keep her from revealing details of their affairs. When I asked Mary Bell this question there was a great deal of movement in the rods and for a moment, I thought they were going to uncross.

QUESTION: If Jimmy Hoffa is buried under Giants Stadium, uncross the rods.

ANSWER: No.

COMMENT: American labor leader and convicted criminal Jimmy Hoffa disappeared on July 30, 1975, from the parking lot of the Machus Red Fox Restaurant in Bloomfield Township, Michigan. He was there to meet two Mafia leaders, Anthony Giacalone from Detroit and Anthony Provenzano from Union City, New Jersey. His disappearance has led to much speculation as to what happened to him. A popular theory is that his body was buried beneath Giants Stadium in New Jersey during its construction. Charles Brandt, a former prosecutor has interviewed Frank Sheeran, a former Mafia hit man and close friend of Hoffa's who claimed that he helped lure Hoffa to a house in northwestern Detroit where he was shot. Brandt claims that

Hoffa's body was taken from the murder scene and possibly driven two minutes away to the Grand Lawn Cemetery, where he was cremated.

QUESTION: If the United States actually landed men on the moon, uncross the rods.

ANSWER: Yes.

COMMENT: Did NASA fake some or all elements of the Apollo moon landings? A number of different hoax theories have been advanced. No one has proposed a complete narrative of how the hoax could have been perpetrated, but instead believers focus on perceived gaps or inconsistencies in the historical record of the missions. I have always believed the 1978 film, *Capricorn One*, in which a fake Mars landing takes place in an Apollo-type craft and the public's general mistrust of the government following Watergate, inspired these theories. Several countries, including the Soviet Union, had the technology to track the Apollo spacecraft and I cannot help but feel that the Russians would have jumped at the opportunity to embarrass the United States during the Cold War if they had evidence that revealed the moon landings to be faked.

QUESTION: If Aaron Kosminski was the serial killer, Jack the Ripper, cross the rods.

ANSWER: Yes.

COMMENT: Jack the Ripper is an alias given to an unidentified serial killer active in the largely impoverished Whitechapel area and adjacent districts of London, England, in the late-nineteenth century. The name is taken from a letter sent to the Central News Agency by someone claiming to be the murderer. The victims were women allegedly earning income as prostitutes. The murders occurred in public or semi-public places at night or toward the early morning, with the victim's throat cut, after which the body was mutilated. Because internal organs were removed from three of the victims, some officials at the time of the murders proposed that the killer possessed anatomical or surgical knowledge. The legend of The Ripper grew through newspapers, owing to the savagery of the attacks and the failure of the police in their attempts to capture the murderer.

When I used the rods to ask Mary Bell the identity of Jack the Ripper, I worked from a list of the reported suspects, including the most popular and the bizarre. The name of Aaron Kosminski was the only one that triggered a response, with the rods crossing slowly. After going through the entire list, I asked the question again using Kosminski's name, and this time the rods reacted quickly to implicate Kosminski. I posed the question a third time after going through the list of Black Dahlia suspects and again the rods responded right away to indicate Kosminski was Jack the Ripper.

Kosminski meets some of the criteria in the general profile of serial killers as outlined by the FBI profilers John Douglas and Robert Ressler, including compulsive masturbation, unsteady employment, and absence of a biological father. He also lived close to the sites of the murders. Additionally, he is the only Ripper suspect ever identified by an eyewitness, although that witness later recanted, possibly because they were not willing to offer testimony against a fellow Jew. He was named a suspect in Chief Constable Melville Macnaghten's memoranda, which stated there were strong reasons for suspecting him, that he "had a great hatred of women, with strong homicidal tendencies." Kosminski was certified insane and admitted to Colney Hatch Lunatic Asylum in February 1891. It has been suggested that Kosminski could not have been The Ripper because he displayed no violent behavior inside the asylum, other than once brandishing a chair at asylum attendants. However, evidence has shown that serial killers often display no violent behavior once they are incarcerated.

QUESTION: If Patrick S. O'Reilly killed Elizabeth Short, known as the Black Dahlia, uncross the rods.

ANSWER: No.

COMMENT: Elizabeth Short was the victim of a gruesome and much-publicized murder. Nicknamed the Black Dahlia, she was found severely mutilated, with her body severed on January 15, 1947, in Leimert Park, Los Angles, California. The still-unsolved murder has been the source of widespread speculation, and several books and films.

When I called upon Mary Bell to identify the killer of the Black Dahlia, I worked off a list of names on the District Attorney's original suspect list and added several names of possible suspects that have been put forth since that time. The only name that generated any kind of response, was Patrick S. O'Reilly. According to Los Angeles district attorney files, Dr. Patrick S. O'Reilly was a medical doctor who knew Elizabeth Short through nightclub owner Mark Hansen. At the time of the murder, O'Reilly was a good friend of Hansen and frequented Hansen's nightclub. Files also state that O'Reilly attended sex parties in Malibu with Hansen. O'Reilly had a history of serious, sexually motivated violent crime. He had been convicted of assault with a deadly weapon for "taking his secretary to a motel and sadistically beating her almost to death for no other reason than to satisfy his sexual desires without intercourse." Further, the files indicated that O'Reilly's right pectoral had been surgically removed, which investigators found similar to the mutilation of Short's body. The first time I mentioned O'Reilly's name the rods jumped with an animated motion and actually uncrossed before crossing slightly. After going through the entire list of names, I asked the question using O'Reilly's name again and the rods uncrossed as before. However, they did not stay uncrossed.

QUESTION: If God created all life on Earth, uncross the rods.

ANSWER: Yes.

COMMENT: The rods responded slowly to this question before uncrossing. There are many theories on how life on Earth started. One theory suggests that the steam from volcanoes formed clouds and it started to rain. After months of rain the oceans formed. Another theory suggests that a meteorite containing frozen H_2O collided with the earth to form the oceans. Some say that life seeded from an extraterrestrial environment. The majority of the world's religions hold that God created all life on earth without further explanation as to how.

QUESTION: If people evolved from lower life forms, cross the rods.

ANSWER: No.

COMMENT: Ever since Charles Darwin, an English naturalist first suggested that species (including humans) evolved through a process of natural selection, a battle has waged between those who support Darwin's theories, and certain elements of the Church who viewed Darwin's work as an attack on the Holy Word of the Bible. This battle culminated in the famous Scopes Monkey Trial, in which authorities charged Tennessee schoolteacher John Scopes with illegally teaching Darwin's theories in his high school biology class.

Conclusion

While I certainly enjoyed asking Mary Bell questions about some of the world's great mysteries, I always knew that the answers I received were not conclusive evidence, and in the end, only raised more questions. I found it interesting that Mary Bell never gave me a false positive when answering. For example, when I asked her to identify Jack the Ripper she only responded to one name.

Do Mary Bell's answers represent the truth? Perhaps one day we will have the technology that allows us to know for certain, but until then, the mysteries remain open to speculation.

GET MORE AT LLEWELLYN.COM

Visit us online to browse hundreds of our books and decks, plus sign up to receive our e-newsletters and exclusive online offers.

- Free tarot readings • Spell-a-Day • Moon phases
- Recipes, spells, and tips • Blogs • Encyclopedia
- Author interviews, articles, and upcoming events

GET SOCIAL WITH LLEWELLYN

Find us on **Facebook**
www.Facebook.com/LlewellynBooks

Follow us on **twitter**
www.Twitter.com/Llewellynbooks

GET BOOKS AT LLEWELLYN

LLEWELLYN ORDERING INFORMATION

Order online: Visit our website at www.llewellyn.com to select your books and place an order on our secure server.

Order by phone:
- Call toll free within the U.S. at 1-877-NEW-WRLD (1-877-639-9753)
- Call toll free within Canada at 1-866-NEW-WRLD (1-866-639-9753)
- We accept VISA, MasterCard, and American Express

Order by mail:
Send the full price of your order (MN residents add 6.875% sales tax) in U.S. funds, plus postage and handling to: Llewellyn Worldwide, 2143 Wooddale Drive Woodbury, MN 55125-2989

POSTAGE AND HANDLING:
STANDARD: (U.S. & Canada)
(Please allow 12 business days)
$25.00 and under, add $4.00.
$25.01 and over, FREE SHIPPING.

INTERNATIONAL ORDERS (airmail only):
$16.00 for one book, plus $3.00 for each additional book.

Visit us online for more shipping options. Prices subject to change.

FREE CATALOG!

To order, call
1-877-NEW-WRLD
ext. 8236
or visit our website